Remarks on the uses of the definitive article in the Greek text of the New Testament, containing many new proofs of the divinity of Christ, from passages which are wrongly translated in the common English version

Sharp, Granville, Whitby, Daniel, Burgess, Thomas

BIBLIOLIFE

Lightning Source UK Ltd.
Milton Keynes UK
UKHW022325010922
408189UK00010B/2078

9 781110 305407

REMARKS

ON THE USES OF THE

DEFINITIVE ARTICLE

IN THE

GREEK TEXT OF THE NEW TESTAMENT,

Containing many New Proofs

OF THE

DIVINITY OF CHRIST,

From Paffages which are wrongly tranflated
in the
COMMON ENGLISH VERSION.

BY GRANVILLE SHARP.

To which is added
AN APPENDIX,

Containing

1. A TABLE OF EVIDENCES OF CHRIST'S DIVINITY,
By Dr. Whitby.

2. A PLAIN ARGUMENT FROM THE GOSPEL HIS-
TORY FOR THE DIVINITY OF CHRIST,
By the former learned Editor.

AND TWO OTHER APPENDIXES,
Added by the Author.

THIRD EDITION.

LONDON:
sold by
VERNOR AND HOOD; F. AND C. RIVINGTON; J. WHITE; AND
J. HATCHARD:
AND L. PENNINGTON, DURHAM.

1803.

ADVERTISEMENT

TO THE

FIRST EDITION.

THE firſt part of the following Remarks, on the uſes of the definitive article in the Greek text of the New Teſtament, was printed in the ſecond Faſciculus of the Muſeum Oxonienſe. A Supplement to the Remarks was at the ſame time promiſed to be publiſhed in the third Faſciculus of the Muſeum. But, as many learned friends concurred with the Editor in thinking that the Remarks contain a very valuable acceſſion to the evidences of Chriſt's divinity, he was unwilling to detain the Supplement, which exemplifies the rules of the Remarks, any longer from the public, and has therefore prevailed on Mr Sharp to permit him to publiſh it with the Remarks. He earneſtly recommends them both to Mr Wakefield's moſt deliberate conſideration.

To Mr Sharp's Remarks and Supplement he has subjoined a plain historical proof of the divinity of Christ, founded on Christ's own testimony of himself, attested and interpreted by his living witnesses and enemies, the Jews, — on the evidence of his trial and crucifixion, — and on the most explicit declarations of the Apostles after the Resurrection of Christ. What appeared to him, on a former occasion,* to be a substantial and unanswerable argument, he has, in this little exercise on the subject, endeavoured to render an easy and popular proof of our Saviour's divinity. It was printed separately for the use of the unlearned part of his parishioners, and is subjoined to this treatise for the convenience of other unlearned readers, and such as have not much considered the subject.

DURHAM, Nov. 1798.

---

* In a sermon on the divinity of Christ. Second edition, 1792.

To GRANVILLE SHARP, Esq.

Dear Sir.

I HAVE great pleaſure in preſenting you with a new Edition of your valuable Tract. That you have very happily and deciſively applied your rule of conſtruction to the correction of the common English verſion of the New Teſtament, and to the perfect eſtablishment of the great doctrine in queſtion, the divinity of Chriſt, no impartial reader, I think, can doubt, who is at all acquainted with the original language of the New Teſtament: I ſay, deciſively applied, becauſe, I ſuppoſe, in all remote and written teſtimony the weight of evidence muſt ultimately depend on the grammatical analogy of the language in which it is recorded. I call the rule yours; for, though it was acknowledged and applied by Beza and others to ſome

of

of the texts alleged by you, yet never so prominently, because singly, or so effectually, as in your remarks.

In the advertisement to the former Edition I wished to excite the attention of a learned and declared enemy to the doctrine of our Saviour's Divinity. But he is no more: and I do not know that he ever expressed, or has left behind him, any opinion on the subject; or that any other Socinian has undertaken to canvass the principle of your Remarks. The public, however, has very lately seen an ample and learned confirmation* of your rule, drawn from a very minute, laborious, and candid, examination of the Greek and Latin Fathers.

I have taken some pains to improve the *plain argument* for Christ's Divinity, which I before subjoined to your Remarks. In this edition I have prefixed to it a *Table of Evidences* by Dr WHITBY, which, I hope, the
younger

* In Six Letters addressed to Granville Sharp, Esq. respecting his Remarks on the uses of the definite article in the Greek Text of the New Testament. London, 1802.

younger part of your readers will find ufeful to them in purfuing the different branches of this moft important fubject; and you, I think, will not difapprove, becaufe it is conducive to the principal purpofe of your Tract.

I am, dear Sir,

With great refpect and efteem,

Your faithful humble Servant,

T. BURGESS.

College, Durham,
March 5, 1802.

PREFACE

to the

THIRD EDITION.

By the Author.

—— o ——

AFTER the author had fent to the prefs
a copy of this work, containing all the corrections and additional notes which are now
printed in this third edition, he received a
printed book, addreffed to himfelf, intituled
" Six more Letters to *Granville Sharp, Efq.*
on his Remarks upon the Ufes of the Article
in the Greek Teftament, by *Gregory Blunt*, Efq."
G. Sharp carefully perufed thefe " *Six more Letters,*" and could not difcover, throughout the
whole of Mr *Blunt's* laborious work, (confift-
ing of 218 pages,) more than *one fingle cenfure* which had any *juft* foundation, viz. that
which

which mentions *G. Sharp's* erroneous quotation*
from the Alexandrian M S. But all the other
cenfures and allegations of Mr *G. Blunt* are fo
evidently *frivolous* and *groundlefs,*† and fome
of them fo *blafphemous*, that they form, altogether, an attack more obvioufly levelled
againft the fupreme dignity and " *divinity of
Chrift*," and againft the *competency* of the *original writers of the New Teftament*, than againft
the Remarks of *G. Sharp*, which are founded
merely on their authority.

Mr *Blunt's* unhappy want of *faith* in the
doctrine of *Chrift's divinity*, (to which he too
plainly alludes when he mentions " *a monftrous
confequence*," p. 48; and " *an abfolute impoffi-
bility*," p. 49 and 70,) together with his *dis-
belief*

---

* Before Mr *Blunt's* book was publifhed, *G. Sharp* had
acknowledged his obligations to another perfon for the
firft difcovery and correction of this *erroneous quotation*, viz.
to a learned writer in the *Britifh Critic*, (fee note in p. 38
and 39,) whofe judicious remarks, publifhed fo long ago
as July, 1802, were evidently known to Mr *Blunt*, for he
has cited them in his own work, (not publifhed till March,
1803,) though he has not thanked that learned writer
for giving him the *firft hint* of *G. Sharp's* error!

† See note, No. 2, in the fourth Appendix, p. 124.

belief even of the exiftence of the *Holy Spirit*,
p. xxii. 70, and 83,) are manifeftly the true
fources of his laboured oppofition to *G. Sharp*,
— nay, the *only foundations*, it feems, that he
has for all his (otherwife) *groundlefs* remarks,
allegations, and cenfures! But, if his un-
guarded affertions had really been true, he
would not have found it neceffary, for the
fupport of his own *groundlefs principles*, fo
ftrenuoufly to decry the authority of the
original writers of the Greek Teftament; and
to endeavour, in the *moft contemptuous* terms,
to depreciate their abilities, by denying their
competency to exprefs themfelves with grammatical *accuracy* or *elegance:* (p. 26, l. 1—11,
and p. 27, l. 19:) calling them " *popular,
loofe, and informal, writers,*" (p. 26,) — " *men,
difqualified, by their rank and education, for*
ELEGANT *writing,*" (p. 34,) — " *more rude
than the moft rude of the Galilæan penmen,*"
(p. 74.) As if he had never read or heard of
the miraculous " *gift of tongues,*" nor of the
pertinent remark of thofe who heard the won-
derful power of expreffion, even *in all languages,* that was then conferred upon thofe

very

very men whom Mr *Blunt* has deemed " *dis-qualified for elegant writing!*" — " ARE NOT ALL THESE THAT SPEAK GALILÆANS?" ('Acts, ii. 7.)

, Neverthelefs, Mr *Blunt* ventures to affert, that the writers of the Englifh Bible " *were much better acquainted with, and much more ftudious of, grammatical niceties than any of the apoftles and evangelifts,*" &c. (p. 26.) — " *Let us appeal to thofe,*" (fays he, in p. 27,) " *who, compared with apoftles and evangelifts, were accuracy itfelf; to thofe who were men of fuperior education, were trained to grammar from their infancy, and wrote in their native lan-guage; none, of which things con be affirmed of the writers of the New Teftament.*"

Now, though this is Mr *Blunt's* own pro-pofal and appeal, yet, when two gentlemen of unexceptionable character in all the points required by himfelf; (except, indeed, in the unreafonable *pride* of pretending, like him, to vie " *with apoftles and evangelifts*" for *accuracy* and abilities;) — men of regular academical education, and both of them juftly eminent for their learning and abilities; — when two
                                                                    fuch

such unexceptionable men have openly declared their conviction of the truth of this *apoſtolical doɛtrine*, "*the Divinity of Chriſt*," contrary to the unhappy prejudices of Mr *Blunt*; the one, (the learned editor of the two firſt editions of this little work,) by citing, in an appendix, ample evidences, from the Holy Scriptures, for "*the Divinity of Chriſt:*" and the other, (the learned writer of the firſt "*Six Letters to Granville Sharp,*") by his full and clear confirmation of the firſt and principal rule of conſtruɛtion, to demonſtrate *the ſame neceſſary doɛtrine*, as ſtated by theſe deſpiſed "*apoſtles and evangeliſts.*" Such worthy examples, by regular academical ſcholars, ought to have occaſioned ſome little reſtraint on the mind of Mr *Blunt:* but, alas! the clear teſtimonies of theſe two learned and reſpeɛtable advocates for *apoſtolic* doɛtrine have had no other effeɛt on the violent oppoſer of it than that of irritating his prejudices, whereby he has been unhappily hurried into the moſt inconſiſtent abuſe and contempt of theſe "*men of ſuperior education*," — the very de-

ſcription

fcription of perfons to whom he himfelf has propofed to appeal!

And as to the author of the rules, *G. Sharp*, who has no fuch literary pretenfions, — not the leaft claim to "*fuperior education*," or to academical acquirements, Mr *Blunt* (confiding, we will fuppofe, in the importance of *his own claffical* abilities) treats him with the moft contemptuous language, and is careful to imprefs on the minds of his readers the degrading trait of G. Sharp's *inferiority of education;* alluding, by frequent repetitions, to his being bred as a mere *tradefman,** *mechanic*, or *manufacturer.†* Whereas, on the other hand, Mr *Blunt* himfelf, being fufficiently fenfible; no doubt, of his own "*fuperior education*,"‡ is manifeftly *inflated*, by the comparifon, to a greater extent and *ftretch* of *felf-confidence* than any human fkin can contain: for, he has *burft* forth into fuch ftrains of *magifterial* importance, and has affumed fuch *inquifitorial* authority

* See Note, No. 4, in the fourth Appendix, p 133.
† See Note, No. 5, in the fourth Appendix, p. 134.
‡ See Note, No. 6, in the fourth Appendix, p. 137.

thority over the fuppofed *tradefman*, as if he were really *refponfible* to his jurifdiction! " *What is your experience?*" (fays he, p. 42.) — " *Wherein does it confift?* — *What does it amount to?*" No culprit was ever more contemptuoufly examined, with fo many hafty queftions all in a.breath. But *G. Sharp* does not wifh to evade thefe imperious demands, howfoever worfhipful Mr *Blunt* may think himfelf in his felf-appointed ftation on the upper bench of *critical* authority. As to the *experience*, therefore, of *G. Sharp*, and, in the firft place, the *experience* acquired by *education*, it was juft like, the *experience* of other *tradef- men* and *manufacturers*, i. e. by no means *claffical*. And, if he afterwards acquired fome little knowledge of *Greek*, he has not prefumed to extend his *experience* beyond the *Greek Teftament*; except now and then by occafional reference to the feveral *Greek* verfions of the Old Teftament, and fometimes alfo to a few *Greek* hiftorians. But, from the *Greek* Teftament, more efpecially, he has been convinced, by *experience*, that the *writings* of thofe eminent perfons, whom the *magifterial* Mr *Blunt*

con-

contemptuoufly calls "*rude Galilæan penmen*,"
as well as the more antient canonical *writings*
of their *Ifraelitifh* countrymen,* are of fo
fuperior a nature, in comparifon with all other
writings, (even with thofe that are deemed
moft eminently *claffical*,) and are fo very
different in their general *idiom* and *peculiarity
of expreffion*, that *rules* drawn from the fyntax
of thefe facred writings,† whether *Hebrew* or
Greek, (for the interpretation, refpectively, of
the *Hebrew* or *Greek* Scriptures,) cannot
reafonably be cenfured for want of conformity
to any *other* writings, either in *fyntax* or *fenti-
ment*, though they may fairly receive confirmation occafionally from *other writings*, as the
learned and modeft writer of the firft *Six
Letters to G. Sharp* has clearly proved by his
candid and judicious felection of examples from
the writings of the *Greek* fathers in defence of
the *firft* and moft important *rule*; and whofe
remarks alfo on the *other* rules had induced G.
Sharp to withdraw an example from his fifth
rule,

---

* See Note, No. 7, in the fourth Appendix, p. 142.
† See Note, No. 8, in the fourth Appendix, p. 143.

rule, and to place it among the *exceptions*, becaufe of the high and refpectable authorities cited by the worthy writer of the firft *Six Letters* in favour of a contrary *interpretation* of that text, and more efpecially becaufe it had been conftrued as a teftimony of *the Divinity of Jefus.* But, if G. Sharp had previoufly feen Mr *Blunt's* " *Six more Letters*," he would not fo readily have made that conceffion; becaufe the *experience* of the *mechanic* is confiderably enlarged fince he examined Mr *Blunt's frivolous* and *groundlefs* objections, not only to the firft rule, but alfo to all the other *rules.* *

For, by the *experience* gained in perufing thefe *Six more Letters,* G. Sharp has difcovered that Mr *Blunt's* unhappy want of *faith* in the neceffary doctrine of " *Chrift's Divinity,*"† is the true caufe of all his miferable *twiftings, ftrainings, fhufflings,* and *fruitlefs endeavours* to evade the " *articular ftraps,*" — " *forcing irons,*" and other *bands* propofed for literary *fecurity* in the *manufacturer's* new-invented *machine,* (as

Mr

---

* See Note, No. 2, in the fourth Appendix, p. 124.

† See Note, No. 3, in the fourth Appendix, p. 131.

Mr *Blunt* calls it,) by which Mr *Blunt* himfelf,
it feems, has been unwarily " *caught and held
willy nilly,*"* notwithftanding his moft violent
and unfair exertions to evade and oppofe it.
So that this fubfequent *experience* of *G. Sharp,*
which he acquired by Mr *Blunt's* forcible *trial*
and *proof* of the *machine,* has convinced him
that even the writings of the *Chriftian Fathers*
do not afford fufficient authority to fet afide
any *rules of fyntax* which are fairly and honeft-
ly formed according to the *general fyntax* of
the *Greek Teftament;* — no, not even for the
purpofe of retaining the *fuppofed* teftimony of
any text whatfoever in favour of our *Lord's
Divinity;* efpecially as that doctrine is abundantly and fufficiently confirmed by a great
multitude of other plain texts, without de-
viating from the *ordinary fyntax* of the *Greek*
Teftament. For, as we are affured that all
Scripture (all the canonical Scripture of the
Jewifh nation †) is given " *by infpiration of God;*"
(2 Tim. iii. 16;) — that " *holy men of God
fpake*

---

* See Note, No. 5, in the fourth Appendix, p. 134.

† See Notes, No. 7 and 8, in the fourth Appendix,
p. 142 to 144.

spake as they were moved by the Holy Ghost;"
(2 Pet. 20, 21;) and not according *to their own
will*, as Mr *Blunt* feems to fuppofe by his
quotation from Dr Whitby, " *Scripiffet ergo
Judas fi hoc voluiffet*;"† and that even thofe
perfons, whom he calls "*rude Galilæan penmen*,"
had an abfolute promife of being endowed
with the moft ample abilities for *teaching*.
" THE HOLY GHOST" (faid our Lord) "*fhall
TEACH you, in the fame hour, what ye ought to
fay*." (Luke, xii. 12; though Mr *Blunt* has
been pleafed to prefer " *the accuracy of our
Englifh tranflators*," p. 20.) And it would
be abfurd to conceive that our *divine* and
infallible inftructor, our bleffed Lord, the light
of the world, fhould promife his difciples the
future guidance of the *Holy Spirit* in terms fo
unqueftionably expreffive of an *actual agency*,
if the *Holy Spirit* was an *imaginary being*, a
mere " *temper*" of the human mind, according
to the *groundlefs* notions of Mr *Blunt!* (p.
xxii. l. 3 from bottom, 70, and 83.) At
another time our Lord faid to thefe *Galilæans*,
" *Thefe*

---

† See Note, No. 9, in the fourth Appendix, p. 144.

"*Thefe things have I fpoken unto you, being prefent with you; but the* HOLY GHOST, *whom the Father will fend in* MY NAME," (for that ineftimable *gift* muft be *afked* in the name of *Jefus,)* "HE WILL TEACH YOU ALL THINGS," (fo that they could not be deficient, as Mr *Blunt* has conceived, in any refpect whatfoever,) "*and* (fhall) *bring all things to your remembrance whatfoever I have faid unto you.*" John, xiv. 25 and 26. But, alas! Mr *Blunt's* rooted prejudices againft "*the divinity of Chrift,*" and his fatal difbelief of the exiftence of *the Holy Spirit,* by which alone he might have been enabled to refift the falfe fuggeftions of *evil fpirits,* are ample and fufficient caufes to be affigned for the *darknefs* of his mind when he charged the Apoftles and Evangelifts with the want of *grammatical* "*accuracy,*" and with want of *ability* to exprefs themfelves with *elegance!*

G. *Sharp,* having thus far fubmitted to the arbitrary demands of Mr *Blunt,* in *freely* declaring the nature of his *experience,* may now feem entitled to demand of Mr *Blunt,* in return, — "*What is your experience? — Wherein does it confift? — What does it amount to?* —

But

But such haughty demands are suitable only to the character of Mr *Blunt* himself; and, indeed, he has precluded the neceſſity of putting any such queſtions about his own *experience*, by venturing, *boldly* and *bluntly*, all at once, to inform us, both *"wherein it doth confiſt,"* and alſo *"what it does amount to,"* — nay, even the ſum total of all the *experience* and knowledge that he has acquired, as he ſays, *"by a diligent and careful ſtudy of the Bible!"* — *"namely,* (ſays he, in p. 171,) *that moral and practical Chriſtianity is the only Chriſtianity contained in the Scriptures."* But, ſurely, this falls very ſhort of what he ought to have *acquired* by his ſtudy of the Bible! — Did he never read, that *"without faith,* it is impoſſible to pleaſe God?"* (Heb. xi. 6.) So that Mr *Blunt's* *"moral and practical Chriſtianity,"* without that neceſſary *faith* and *knowledge*, which the Scripture clearly *teaches*, is not worthy to be called *Chriſtianity* at all! For, even Pagans and Unbelievers, from the *natural knowledge of good and evil* in man, pretend to virtue and morality; and *Julian*, the Apoſtate, the hero of Mr *Gibbon*, would

---

* See note p. xxxviii

would have contended as ftiffly for the *morality* *and practical virtue* of the worſhippers of *Ju- piter* and *Hercules* as our modern *Unitarians* can poſſibly do, or any other ſectaries of *merely nominal* Chriſtians, who learn nothing at all from the Holy Scriptures but *morality* alone !

This pretence to *morality*, when adopted ſe- parately from the neceſſity of acquiring *faith* and *knowledge*, is manifeſtly the baneful doctrine of *works*, whereon the *Papiſts* build that noto- rious branch of Popiſh ſuperſtition, *ſupererero- gation*; a doctrine not leſs unſcriptural and ab- ſurd than that of *tranſubſtantiation*, which Mr *Blunt* has ſo earneſtly and repeatedly preſſed upon *G. Sharp*, (in the true *Papiſtical* way, under a *cloak* of contrary pretenſions,) in his vain compariſon between that and the doctrine of the Trinity; inſinuating, that he who ad- mits the one muſt needs admit the other! Now, with reſpect to the doctrine of *tranſub- ſtantiation*, — unleſs Mr *Blunt* and his friends, the *Popiſh* and *Socinian* advocates for it, (ſee the *Unitarian* tracts to which he refers us in a note at p. 151,) can ſhew, by plain proofs of Holy Scripture, that our Lord's inſtitution of

the

the facrament of *bread* and *wine* was not de-
figned merely for the purpofes univerfally acknowledged by the primitive churches of the
three firft centuries, and by the *reformed churches*,
or true *Catholic Church*, of the prefent day, but
for feveral *other different* purpofes, as that of
conftituting the outward fymbol of *bread* to be
fet up as an object of *public worship and adoration*,—that of referving the bread, confecrated
on Eafter-Day, for a whole year, as an infallible *charm* for various purpofes, — and that
of making every mafs a *new facrifice*, inftead of
the *commemoration*, only, commanded by our
Lord, of *the one* efficacious facrifice *once offered* ;*
befides the grofs prefumption of altering our
Lord's inftitution, by denying the cup to the
laity, though our Lord had exprefly com-

---

* "Knowing that Chrift, being raifed from the dead,
DIETH NO MORE; death hath no more dominion over
him; for, in that he died he died unto fin, ONCE, but in
that he liveth he liveth unto God." Rom. vi. 9 and 10.
— "And as it is appointed unto men ONCE TO DIE, but
after this the judgement: fo Chrift was ONCE OFFERED
to bear the fins of many," &c. Heb. ix. 27 and 28.
"For *Chrift* alfo hath ONCE SUFFERED for fins,"
&c. 1 Pet. iii. 18.

manded,

manded, — "DRINK YE ALL OF IT, *for this is my blood of the new covenant,*"† (της καινης δια-θηκης,) inftead of the abrogated fign of the *old covenant* circumcifion,) "*which is fhed for many, for the remiffion of fins :*" "*But, I fay unto you, I will not drink henceforth of* THIS FRUIT OF THE VINE *until that day that I drink it new with you in my Father's kingdom.*" Matth. xxvi. 27 to 29. — The commemoration of our Lord's *blood* is more particularly defcribed by St Paul, 1 Cor. xi. 25 to 29. "*This cup is the* NEW COVENANT *in my* BLOOD: *this do ye, as oft as ye drink* (it) IN REMEMBRANCE *of me :*" fo that the *wine* was the *outward fign* only of our Lord's *blood*, to be fo taken *in remembrance* of him. And in four fucceeding verfes the drinking of the cup is exprefsly mentioned, jointly with the *eating* of the BREAD, as of *equal* importance, by being *equally* commanded ; and, fo far from any *change of fubftance*, or *tranfubftantiation*, taking place, that our Lord himfelf, according to St Matthew's account, called the contents of the cup "*this fruit of the vine*," even after his

euchariftical

---

† See note p. xxxviii.

euchariſtical confecration of it by *thankſgiving,*
(*ευχαριςησας.*) So that unleſs all this groſs *inno-*
vation from the *euchariſtical* ceremony, ordained
by Chriſt, can be plainly proved, either by
Papiſts or *Socinians,* to be confiſtent with the
faith and *practice* of the Apoſtles and the primitive church, it furely does *not* ſtand upon the
ſame foundation as the generally-received doctrine of the primitive church, concerning the
" *divinity of Chriſt,*" and actual exiſtence and
divinity of the Holy Spirit; and muſt therefore
be condemned with an *anathema,* even if it
had been taught by *one* of the Apoſtles, (contrary to the general evidence of the reſt,) or
by " *an angel from Heaven !* (Gal. i. 8 and 9.)
And, in like manner, Mr *Blunt's* declaration,
that " *morality, and practical Chriſtianity is the*
only Chriſtianity contained in the Scriptures," is
furely an entire excluſion of the true Chriſtian's
belief or *faith*; an excluſion which manifeſtly
favours the Popiſh SUPEREROGATION of works,
whereby a man may lay up ſuch a *treaſure of*
his own merits as may entitle him, after his
death, to a *Papal* canonization as a SAINT of
the *Roman* church, whereby he becomes a

Popiſh

Popiſh object of *religious worſhip* and prayer, for his *mediation*, inſtead of the only " ONE MEDIATOR *between God and Man*," (1 Tim. ii. 5.) And Mr *Blunt* ſeems not at all to be aware that this deceitful *Popiſh* atonement, by the pretended *mediation of dead ſaints*, muſt be equally efficacious as that of the *one mediator*, if the *Socinian blaſphemy* was really true, that Chriſt " was a *mere man*, and *nothing more* ;" for in this, as in many other points, the *Papal* and *Socinian* tenets are intimately and cloſely combined together for the perverſion of the true primitive doctrines of *Chriſtianity*, notwithſtanding the imaginary differences which are generally ſuppoſed to exiſt between theſe two notorious ſects of *heretics*, and their open oppoſition and external contempt of each other. This has been remarkably demonſtrated in a learned work of Mr *Jameſon*, printed at Edinburgh, in 1702, entituled " *Roma Racoviana et Racovia Romana*," * which Mr *Blunt*, if he

pleaſes,

---

* Id eſt *Papiſtarum* et *Sociniſtarum*, in plurimis, iiſque maximi momenti, religionis ſuæ capitibus, plena et exacta harmonia : in quâ, unam eandemque utriuſque religionis

eſſe

pleafes, may add to the propofed new edition of the *Unitarian tracts*, to demonftrate the intimate connection between their *two churches.*

Mr *Blunt* himfelf informs us, in a note, (p. 146,) "that the *Papifts have not only confeffed, but contended, that the Trinity cannot be proved by Scripture:*" and he cites for this a *Popifh* writer, *Sandius*, and alfo the *Unitarian tracts*; and in notes, at p. 148 and 149, cites nearly the fame doctrine from the *Popifh* writer, *Petavius*, and from his own favourite *Socinian* writer, *Taylor*, the author of *Ben Mordecai!*

Thus far it feems obvious, that the *Papifts* conform to the *Socinian* notions againft the *Trinity*; and Mr *Blunt*, in return for this fociable degree of conformity, argues as ftoutly as the *Papifts* for the *Popifh* doctrine of *tranfub-*

---

effe animam et medullam clariffimè oftenditur; unum eundemque Spiritum pariter in utraque Apoftafia regnare evincitur; utriufque fectæ αυτοκαλαχϱισις latè declaratur; fimpliciores, adverfus eorum impetus et technas muniuntur; S. literarum, in impletis vaticiniis, adverfus *fcepticos* et *atheo.*, veritas, et divinitas demonftratur; haud pauca, denique, Chriftianæ theologiæ amanti proficua oppidò toti. paffim operi infperguntur."

ftantiation,

ftantiation, (in p. 151 and 166,) in his comparifon between that falfe *notion* and the doctrine of the *Trinity* : and all this in the true *Papiftical* or *Jacobinical* way, under a cloak of *contrary pretenfions*, to difguife his defire of favouring that *Popifh error!*

In p. 168, Mr *Blunt* charges G. *Sharp* with having, "*for a while at leaft*," forgotten "that *love* of the brotherhood, and *charity* towards all mankind, which is the characteriftic of a true Chriftian, and of having turned (his) back on the maxim of doing to others as (he) would that others fhould do unto (him)." In return to this very ferious charge G. *Sharp* requefts Mr *Blunt* to believe what he now afferts with great fincerity, viz. that his *ufual* feverity, in cenfuring the *doctrines* either of ROMAN CATHOLICS or of SOCINIANS, was never occafioned by any the leaft want of *charity* to the *perfons* or *individuals* of either perfuafion, but, on the contrary, was always exerted with the kindeft intentions, to warn them of the extreme danger of their refpective errors.

With refpect to the *Socinians*, G. *Sharp* has produced, many years ago, fuch ample proofs,

in

in his tract on the *Nature of Man*, of " *the divinity of Chriſt*," and of " *the Holy Spirit*," and more eſpecially of that doctrine which Mr *Blunt* denies, in p. 133, l. 5; p. 136, l. 10; and p. 165, l. 24; that the title of *Jehovah* is applied to *Chriſt*, and alſo to the *Holy Spirit*; that, if Mr *Blunt* will fairly examine theſe proofs, he will find it impoſſible to ſet them aſide without an equal perverſion of the Holy Scripture from whence they are drawn. *G. S.* would not make ſuch a confident aſſertion, if he had not ſubmitted that work, previous to its publication, to the careful examination of a very learned and conſcientious *Socinian*, who had quitted holy orders, and a good living in the *Church of England*, merely on account of ſome prejudices he had imbibed in favour of the *Unitarian* doctrines; and *G. S.* has ample reaſon to believe, that he would not have deſerted the *Church of England* if he had previouſly been at all aware that any ſuch proofs exiſted; for he did not make the leaſt objection to any of them, but only requeſted ſome few alterations of *expreſſion*, to leſſen the ſeverity of cenſure againſt the *Socinians*. And at another time

a very learned *Socinian* Clergyman having addreſſed to *G. Sharp* a *private letter*, containing
many laboured arguments againſt " *the divinity
of Chriſt*," *G. Sharp* returned ſuch proofs of
the CONTRARY DOCTRINE, that the learned
and able diſputant was obliged entirely to
change the ground and poſition of his former
arguments, and to advance again with new pro-
poſitions, in a ſecond letter; which alſo *G. Sharp*
fully anſwered, indeed, but not in ſufficient time
for the peruſal of the candid inquirer; whoſe
death will be ever remembered by *G. Sharp*
with regret, through the conſideration of his
own natural ſlowneſs, or, perhaps, want of ſufficient exertion (though he is not conſcious of
any wilful neglect) to return ſuch a timely
anſwer as might have been uſeful to his ſoli-
citous correſpondent!

Though the recital of ſuch circumſtances
may ſubject *G. Sharp*, with too much appearance of probability, to the invidious charges of
vanity, and even of *boaſting*, yet he would wil-
lingly ſubmit in ſilence to ſuch charges, pro-
vided his *true motive* for mentioning them
ſhould prove effectual, viz. that of exciting
in

in Mr *Blunt* a defire to examine more carefully
and ferioufly the tendency of his own profeffed
principles, *the want of faith in Chrift*, and in
the *Holy Spirit*: for, if Mr *Blunt's* affertions
were true, that the latter is only an *imaginary
being*, it would follow, of courfe, that *man*, the
only being in God's creation which really ftands
in continual need of the guidance and protection of the *Holy Spirit*, would be miferably *dif-
armed* of the moft effectual promifed means of
refifting his moft dangerous enemies, the *affid-
uous*, though *filent*, invaders of his foul; fo that
he muft be eafily conquered and *led captive*
into the moft deplorable *flavery* both of body
and mind: for, without the *Spirit of God*, there
can be no true *liberty*; and therefore G. *Sharp*,
as a fincere friend to *liberty*, cannot view the
profeffed principles of Mr *Blunt* and his *Unitarian* brethren with indifference, nay, not without the moft anxious concern and intereft for
their fafety and welfare, (whatever Mr *Blunt*
may think of his want of *charity*,) knowing, for
a certainty, that their moft valuable *citizenfhip*,
in the true *Catholic Church*, or *univerfal communion of faints*, (either in that branch of it which
is

is ftill *militant here on earth*, or in that other moft numerous and glorious part of it which, in fpite of all the malice of *Pagan*, *Arian*, and *Popifh*, perfecutors, is now triumphant with their *Lord*, in Heaven,) cannot poffibly exift without the *univerfal communion of the* HOLY SPIRIT, that promifed *participation of the Divine nature* to the *nature of man*, in which the true *unity* of the *city of God*, our moft ineftimable *citizenfhip*, muft neceffarily confift !

It is *not*, therefore, through any *vanity* or fpirit of *boafting*, that *G. Sharp* has recited fome circumftances of his former communications with *Unitarians*, but really for the fake of Mr *Blunt's* own true intereft and welfare ; and if, either under his *real* or *feigned* name, he will call on *G. Sharp*, he will certainly find no occafion to complain of any *want of charity* in his moft earneft endeavours to warn him of his danger, to fatisfy his objections, and remove his difficulties.

For, if he will but ferioufly confider what contemptuous expreffions he has ufed againft *Chrift*, (p. 48, 49, 71, 110, 136, 138, 140, 144, 150, 151, 153, 154, 160, 161, 164, and 173,)

173,) and againſt the *Holy Spirit !* (p. xxii. 70, 83, &c.) he muſt ſurely be convinced that the antient *apoſtates,* mentioned by the Apoſtle to the Hebrews, x. 29, could not, by any outward profeſſion of doctrine, have been more guilty of "*treading under foot the Son of God,*" and of doing "*deſpite unto the Spirit of Grace,*" than he himſelf has really been, in the fulleſt extent of thoſe impieties! The former *apoſtates,* indeed, were deemed worthy of a " *much ſorer puniſhment* than thoſe that *deſpiſed Moſes' law, and died without mercy*; (compare the 28th and 29th verſes;) but, as the Apoſtle has added, in the two next verſes,—"*for we know him that hath ſaid, vengeance* (belongeth) *unto me, I will recompence, ſaith the Lord,*" &c.—we are thereby aſſured, that the " *much ſorer puniſhment,*" there denounced, is not of a *temporal* kind, like that inflicted *by man on the deſpiſers of Moſes' law :* for, as we are now under a *milder* and *more perfect* ſyſtem of revelation, we muſt not (after the manner of the Church of *Rome,* though her doctrines are deemed ſo weighty and unanſwerable by Mr *Blunt)* preſume to perſecute with *fire and ſword* on account of religion, or

to

to *burn men alive* for their opinions, as she has done! These are proofs only that the *Roman Church* herself *hath long ceased to be Christian,* though she has assumed the title of *Catholic Church,* to the exclusion of all other churches. But her true character was foreseen by the beloved Apostle, who has represented her as seated on the *scarlet*-coloured beast of *temporal* power, *drunk with the* BLOOD *of the Saints* (note,* No. 10) *and with the* BLOOD *of the Martyrs of* JESUS ! But the members of the true *Catholic Church* are restrained, by the principles of their faith, from opposing either *Popish or Socinian heretics* with any other weapon than the *two-edged sword of God's Word,* and from wishing to extirpate and dissolve them with any other sort of *heat* than the purifying *fire of truth,* accompanied with hearty wishes and prayers, that a timely repentance may avert the vengeance !

The aweful warning which was given to an eminent person, who for some time unhappily opposed the necessary doctrine of *Christ's divinity,* not less *violently* than Mr *Blunt* himself,

seems

* Fourth Appendix, p. 147.

feems as peculiarly applicable to the *present*
as to the *former* occasion; and, as the sentence
originally proceeded from *supreme Authority*,
the citing of it now must not be considered as
having the least reference to the facetious sar-
casm which Mr *Blunt* has affected throughout
his work, (*i. e.* the trite contrast between *Sharp*
and *Blunt*,) for, the true application of it is
certainly of a much more serious nature; because it shews the extreme difficulty and danger of opposing the divine dignity of our
bleffed Redeemer, — σκληρον σοι προς κενδρα λακ-
ηζειν, (Acts, ix. 5, xxvi. 14:) — and a man
who has wrote and published such degrading
and contemptuous expressions against the *divinity of Chrift*, as are contained in Mr *Blunt's*
book, surely, has not less cause for "*fear and
trembling*," than *Saul* had, on his supernatural
conversion; nor less need, apparently, to be
"*led by the hand*," and instructed, (Acts, xxii.
11 to 16,) until his *eyes* and *understanding* are
opened to the bright and irresistible evidence,
throughout the Holy Scriptures, of Chrift's
supreme dignity.

Note transferred from p. xxiii.

* What kind of *faith* is here to be underſtood, may clearly be known by the general topics of this epiſtle ; but, more eſpecially, by thoſe in the two preceding chapters, and in the following chapter ; for, the objeçts of our *faith* and *hope* are ſtated in them all. See Heb. ix. 14 to 18 ; x. 9 to 15, and 28 to 30 ; (wherein *vengeance* is denounced againſt him " *who hath trodden under foot the Son of God,*" &c. " *and have done deſpite unto the Spirit of Grace* ;) and chap. xii. 2, wherein our Lord *Jeſus* is expreſſly called " *the Author*" (or Leader, αρχηγον) " *and finiſher of our* FAITH." Τον της πιστεως αρχηγον και τελιωτην Ιησυν, &c.

Note transferred from p. xxvi.

† It is, at the ſame time, a *new teſtament*, (as well as a *new covenant*,) of which 'Chriſt, by his death, was the *teſtator*. See Heb. ix. 15 to 18.

Note transferred from p. xxv. l. 3 from bottom.

(—— the groſs preſumption of altering ‡ our Lord's inſtitution, by denying the cup to the laity, &c.)

‡ Deut. xii. 32.—" *What thing ſoever I command you,* " *obſerve to do it : thou ſhalt not add thereto, nor diminiſh* " *from it.*"—A continual breach of this COMMAND OF GOD (in either " *adding to,*" or " *diminiſhing from,*" almoſt every *divine ordinance*) is a notorious mark of the *apoſtacy* of the *Roman* church, whatſoever her *Socinian* advocates may think of it ! The *exorciſms* of water, &c. for *Baptiſm*, and alſo for purpoſes *not commanded*, are abominable açts of *ſorcery !* See the deteſtable forms in the " *Miſſale Romanum,*" under the heads of " *Benedictio Fontis,*" (p. 273 to 285,) and " *Ordo ad faciendam aquam benedictam,*" (p. cxxvi to cxxix.) Plantin. edit. Antwerp, 1682. But the time of her judgement is *now* very near at hand ! (See Note, No. 10, 4th Appendix, p. 147 and 148.)

CONTENTS.

CONTENTS.

RULE I.

When two perſonal nouns of the ſame caſe are connected by the copulative και, if the former has the definitive article, and the latter has not, they both relate to the ſame perſon . . . .

EXAMPLES.

Common Verſion.

1. The God and Father of our Lord.
2. To God, even the Father.

Corrected Verſion.	Common Verſion.
3. In the kingdom of Chriſt, even of God.	In the kingdom of Chriſt, and of God.
4. According to the grace of Jeſus Chriſt, cur God and Lord.	According to the grace of our God, and the Lord Jeſus Chriſt.

Corrected

Corrected Version.	*Common Version.*
5. Before Jesus Christ, the God and Lord; *or,* our God and Lord : *for, the definite article has sometimes the power of a passive pronoun.*	Before God, and the Lord Jesus Christ.
6. The glorious appearing of our great God and Saviour Jesus Christ.	The glorious appearing of the great God, and our Saviour Jesus Christ.
7. Through the righteousness of Jesus Christ, our God and Saviour.	Through the righteousness of God, and our Saviour Jesus Christ.
8. And denying our only Master, God, and Lord, Jesus Christ.	And denying the only Lord God, and our Lord Jesus Christ.

RULE II.

RULE III.

· RULE IV.

RULE V.

RULE VI.

A

LETTER

TO THE

Rev. Mr ————,

CONCERNING THE USES OF THE GREEK ARTICLE
ὁ IN THE NEW TESTAMENT.

═══════

Old Jewry, London, 10*th June,* 1778.

Dear Sir,

WHEN I look upon the date of your laſt obliging letter, I am much aſhamed that I have ſo long neglected to acknowledge the receipt of it. The truth is, I began a letter a few days afterwards; but, recollecting that I had written on the ſame ſubject (viz. the uſe of the Greek article ὁ and copulative ϰαι) to a very learned friend, at a great diſtance in the country, I was willing to wait for his anſwer, leſt it ſhould oblige me to make any alterations in my rules; and ſo, indeed, it has proved; for, he objected to my firſt rule,

B   (as

(as it was then ftated,) and has cited feveral exceptions to it, which he thought fufficient to fet it entirely afide: but this, I am convinced, is going too far, and would be an injury to truth. The ufe, therefore, which I have made of my friend's objeſtions, has been, to correſt my rule, and add to it fuch limitations as might include the feveral exceptions cited by my learned friend, as well as others that are fimilar to them.

The waiting for my friend's anfwer, and the neceffary correſtions in confequence of it, together with a variety of other engagements, have prevented me from complying with your requeft fo foon as I could have wifhed; but I fhall now fubmit to your confideration and candour the rules in queftion, and beg that you will be pleafed to favour me with whatever examples may occur in the courfe of your reading, either as exceptions to invalidate the *firſt rule*, or as proofs to eftablifh and confirm it. The reafon of my recommending the firft rule more particularly to your attention, is, becaufe it is of much more confequence than any of

the

the reſt, as it will enable us (if the truth of
it be admitted) to correct the tranſlation of
ſeveral important texts in the preſent Engliſh
verſion of the New Teſtament, in favour of
a fundamental article of our church, which
has, of late, been much oppoſed and traduced;
I mean the belief that our Lord Jeſus Chriſt
is truly God.

RULE I.

When the copulative και *connects two nouns of
the ſame caſe,* [*viz. nouns (either ſubſtantive
or adjective, or participles) of perſonal deſcription reſpecting office, dignity, affinity, or connection, and attributes, properties, or qualities, good
or ill,*] *if the article* ὁ, *or any of its caſes, precedes the firſt of the ſaid nouns or participles,
and is not repeated before the ſecond noun or
participle, the latter always relates to the ſame
perſon that is expreſſed or deſcribed by the firſt
noun or participle:* i. e. it denotes a farther
deſcription of the firſt-named perſon; as, —
και εθεραπευσεν αυτον, ώςε ΤΟΝ τυφλον ΚΑΙ κωφον και
λαλειν και βλεπειν. Mat. xii. 22. And, again,

B 2   Ευλογητος

Ευλογητος Ὁ Θεος ΚΑΙ Πατηρ τε Κυριε ἡμων Ιησε Χριςε, Ὁ Πατηρ των οικτιρμων ΚΑΙ Θεος πασης παρακλησεως. 2 Cor. i. 3. This laſt ſentence contains two examples of the firſt rule. See alſo in 2 Cor. xi. 31, Ὁ Θεος ΚΑΙ Πατηρ τε Κυριε ἡμων Ιησε Χριςου οιδεν, &c. Alſo in Eph. vi. 21, Τυχικος Ὁ αγαπητος αδελφος ΚΑΙ πιςος διακονος εν Κυριῳ. Alſo in Heb. iii. 1, κατανοησαλε ΤΟΝ αποςολον ΚΑΙ αρχιερεα της ὁμολογιας ἡμων Ιησεν Χριςον, &c. See alſo in 2 Pet. ii. 20, εν επιγνωσει ΤΟΥ Κυριε ΚΑΙ Σωληρος Ιησε Χριςε, &c. And again, in 2 Pet. iii. 2, και της των αποςολων ἡμων ινλολης, ΤΟΥ Κυριε ΚΑΙ Σωτηρος. And again, in 2 Pet. iii. 18, Αυξανετε δε εν χαριλι και γνωσει ΤΟΥ Κυριε ἡμων ΚΑΙ Σωληρος Ιησε Χριςε. αυλῳ ἡ δοξα και νυν και εις ἡμεραν αιωνς, αμην. - Alſo in Philippians, iv. 20, Τῳ δε Θεῳ ΚΑΙ Πατρι ἡμων ἡ δοξα, &c. In Rev. xvi. 15, μακαρις Ὁ γρηγορων ΚΑΙ τηρων τα ἱματια αυτε, ἱνα μη γυμνος περιπαλῃ, &c. And in Col. ii. 2, εις επιγνωσιν τε μυςηριε ΤΟΥ Θεε ΚΑΙ Παλρος και τε Χριςε*, εν ᾧ εισι παλλες ὁι θησαυροι της σοφιας, &c. And in 1 Theſ. iii. 11, Αυλος δε Ὁ Θεος ΚΑΙ Πατηρ ἡμων

---

* The diſtinction of perſons mentioned in this ſentence is preſerved by the inſertion of the article τε before Χριςε, which had been omitted before παλρος.

ἡμων και ὁ Κυριος ἡμων Ιησους Χριςος, καῖευθυναι την
ὁδον ἡμων προς ὑμας. This folemn ejaculation
for the divine direction is addreffed jointly to
the God and Father, and to our Lord Jefus;*
(fo that here is good authority for offering up
prayers to Chrift, which fome have lately oppofed;) and the diftinction of the perfons is
preferved (as in the laft example) by again inferting the article ὁ before Κυριος, which had
been omitted before Πατηρ. The apoftle James
alfo ufed the fame mode of expreffion, θρησκεια
καθαρα και αμιανῖος παρα Τῳ Θεῳ ΚΑΙ Παῖρι ἀυῖη εςιν,
επισκεπῖεθαι ορφανας και χηρας εν τη θλιψει αυῖων,
&c. James, i. 27. And there are at leaft a
dozen other places, (viz. Rom. xv. 6. 1 Cor.

B 3   xv.

---

* This text is clearly a fupplication to Chrift for pro-
vidential affiftance; and, being addreffed to him *jointly* with
God the Father, moft certainly amounts to *fupreme worfhip*, becaufe the direction of Providence belongs to God
alone: fo that a prayer for it, addreffed to Chrift, were he
merely a minifter and difpenfer of God's providence,
and not alfo truly God, would be utterly unlawful:
and more efpecially fo if fuch an inferior difpenfer of
providence (one that was not truly God) was to be addreffed jointly with the heavenly Father; for, that would
be blafphemous.

xv. 24. Gal. i. 4. Ephef. v. 20. Col. i. 3 and
12.* and iii. 17. 1 Thef. i. 3. 1 Thef. iii. 13.
2 Thef. ii. 16. James, iii. 9. Rev. i. 6.) wherein " *the God and Father*" is mentioned exactly
according to this rule; and there is no exception or inftance of the like mode of expreffion,
that I know of, which neceffarily requires
a conftruction different from what is here
laid down, EXCEPT the nouns be *proper names*,
or *in the plural number*; in which cafes
there are many exceptions; though there are
not wanting examples, even of plural nouns,
which are expreffed exactly agreable to this
rule.

As the examples which I have annexed to
my firft rule confift of texts, wherein the
fenfe is fo plain that there can be no con-
troverfy concerning the particular perfons
to whom the feveral nouns are applicable, it
will be thought, I hope, that I have already
cited a fufficient number of them to authenti-
cate and juftify the rule. There are feveral
other

---

* Some copies have not the words θιῳ και in this twelfth
verfe; but only τῳ πατρι τῳ ικανωσαντι; in which laft cafe
this verfe affords an example only of the fecond rule.

other texts wherein the mode of expreſſion
is exactly ſimilar, and which therefore do
neceſſarily require a conſtruction agreeable
to the ſame rule; though the preſent Engliſh
verſion has unhappily rendered them in a
different ſenſe, and has thereby concealed,
from the mere *Engliſh* reader, many ſtriking
proofs *concerning the Godhead* (περι " της Θεοτητος,"
Col. ii. 9.) of our Lord and Saviour, Jeſus
Chriſt. The rules which follow are intended
only to illuſtrate the *particularity* of the
ſeveral ſentences which fall under the *firſt*
rule, by ſhewing, in *other* ſentences, the different ſenſes that are occaſioned by adding,
omitting, or repeating, the article, as well
with the copulative as *without* it.

RULE II.

A repetition of the article before the ſecond
noun, if the copulative be omitted, will have the
ſame effect and power: for, it denotes a farther
deſcription of the ſame perſon, property, or
thing, that is expreſſed by the firſt noun; as in
the following examples: — και ηγαλλιασε το
πνευμα μου επι Τῳ Θεῳ Τῳ Σωτηρι μυ, Luke, 1. 47.

και ην αυτω κεχρηματισμενον ὑπο ΤΟΥ Πνευματος ΤΟΥ ἁγιε, &c. Luke, ii. 26. ιδε Ὁ αμνος τε Θεε Ὁ αιρων την ἁμαρ]ιαν τε κοσμε, John, i. 29. οιδαμεν ὁτι οὑτος εςιν αληθως Ὁ Σω]ηρ τε κοσμε, Ὁ Χριςος, John, iv. 42. ὁ μη τιμων τον Ὑιον, ου τιμα ΤΟΝ πατερα ΤΟΝ πεμψαν]α αυ]ον, John, v. 23. εργαζεσθε μη ΤΗΝ βρωσιν ΤΗΝ απολλυμενην, αλλα ΤΗΝ βρωσιν ΤΗΝ μενεσαν εις ζωην αιωνιον, ἡν ὁ Ὑιος τε ανθρωπε ὑμιν δωσει· τε]ον γαρ Ὁ Πα]ηρ εσφραγιςεν Ὁ Θεος, John, vi. 27. This verſe contains three examples. Ταυ]α δε γεγραπ]αι ινα πιςευση]ε, ὁτι Ὁ Ιησε ςεςιν Ὁ Χριςος Ὁ Ὑιος τε Θεε, &c. John, xx. 31. Ὁ δε Θεος της ειρηνης Ὁ αναγαγων εκ νεκρων ΤΟΝ ποιμενα των προβα]ων ΤΟΝ μεγαν* εν αἱμα]ι

διαθηκης

---

* The apoſtle, in this text, expreſsly calls our Lord Jeſus Chriſt " *the* Great SHEPHERD OF THE SHEEP," τον ποιμενα των προβα]ων τον μεγαν: and the apoſtle Peter entitles him " THE CHIEF SHEPHERD," ὁ αρχιποιμην, 1 Pet. v. 4, which compare with Pſalm xxiii. 1. " JEHO- " VAH *is my* SHEPHERD," and with Iſaiah, xl. 9, 10, 11; " *O Zion that bringeth good tidings*," &c. " *ſay unto the ci-* " *ties of Judah, behold* YOUR GOD! *Behold the Lord* JE- " HOVAH *will come in mighty (power), and* HIS *arm ſhall* " *rule for him: behold* HIS *reward is with him, and* HIS *work* " *before him.* HE" (i.e. the Lord JEHOVAH) " *ſhall* " *feed* HIS *flock like a* SHEPHERD: *he ſhall gather the lambs*

" *with*

διαθηκης αιωνιου, ΤΟΝ κυριον ἡμων Ιησουν καθαρτισαι ὑμας, &c. Heb. xiii. 20. This sentence also contains three examples.

GENERAL EXCEPTION.

Except when genitive cases depend on one another in succession; as, ει δε και εςι κεκαλυμμενον το ευαγγελιον ἡμων, εν τοις απολλυμενοις εςι κεκαλυμμενον, εν οἱς ὁ Θεος τ8 αιωνος τ8τ8 ετυφλωσε τα νοηματα των απιςων, εις το μη αυγασαι αυτοις τον φωτισμον ΤΟΥ ευαγγελι8 ΤΗΣ δοξης ΤΟΥ Χρις8 ὁς ες̄ιν εικων ΤΟΥ

"with his arm," &c. &c. To explain this still farther, the prophet Ezekiel foretold that "all shall have one Shepherd," Ezekiel, xxxvii. 24. And Christ himself expressly acknowledged that eminent pastoral character, saying, "I am the good Shepherd;" ὁ ποιμην ὁ καλος, "and I know MY sheep and am known of MINE." (John, x. 14.) And a little farther (v. 27) our Lord mentions the true mark by which his flocks are known, viz. that of hearing his voice: (compare with 95th Psalm.) "My sheep" (said our Lord) "hear my voice, and I know them; and they follow me, "and I give unto them eternal life," &c. which power of giving eternal life cannot be an attribute of any person that is not truly God, and one with Jehovah or the heavenly Father, as in the 30th verse he is expressly declared to be: "I and my Father are one," ἑν εσμεν, we are one; in which brief expression both the plurality and the unity of the two persons are unquestionably asserted.

ΤΟΥ Θεɐ ΤΟΥ αορατɐ, 2 Cor. iv. 3. And, again, ἱνα παρακληθωσιν ἁι καρδιαι αυτων συμϐιϐασϑεντων εν αγαπη και εις παντα πλɐτον ΤΗΣ πληροφοριας ΤΗΣ συνεσεως, εις επιγνωσιν ΤΟΥ μυϛηριɐ ΤΟΥ Θεɐ και Πατρος και τɐ Χριϛɐ, &c. Coloſſ. ii. 2.

RULE III.

And the omiſſion of the copulative between two or more nouns (of the ſame caſe) of perſonal deſcription or application, even without the article before the ſecond noun, will have the ſame effeƐ: viz. will denote a farther deſcription of the ſame perſon, property, or thing, that is ex-preſſed by the firſt noun; as in the following examples. Πεϖοιθας τε σεαυτον ΟΔΗΓΟΝ ειναι τυφλων, ΦΩΣ των εν σκοτει, ΠΑΙΔΕΥΤΗΝ αφρονων, ΔΙΔΑΣΚΑΛΟΝ νηϖιων, ΕΧΟΝΤΑ την μορφωσιν της γνωσεως και της αληθειας εν τῳ νομῳ, Rom. ii. 19, 20.

Ευχαριϛɐντες παντοτε ὑπερ παντων εν ονοματι τɐ ΚΥΡΙΟΥ ἡμων ΙΗΣΟΥ ΚΡΙΣΤΟΥ, τῳ Θεῳ και Πατρι· ὑποτασσομενοι αλληλοις εν φοϐῳ* Χριϛɐ, Epheſ. v. 20,

---

* Εν φοϐῳ Χριϛɐ. In the modern printed editions the reading is εν φοϐῳ Θεɐ, but in the Complutenſian and ſeveral of the oldeſt editions it is εν φοϐῳ Χριϛɐ; as alſo in the Alexandrian and other old MSS. as well as the antient verſions, and the citations of the Fathers: for which ſee Wetſtein's

20, 21. ΠΑΥΛΟΣ, ΔΟΥΛΟΣ Θε8, ΑΠΟΣΤΟΛΟΣ δε ΙΗΣΟΥ, &c. Tit. i. i. Παυλος Απο5ολος Ιησ8 Χριστου κατ' επιταγην* Θε8 σωτηρος ἡμων, και κυρι8 Ιησ8 Χρι58 της ελπιδος ἡμων, 1 Tim. i. 1.

RULE IV.

Yet it is otherwise when the nouns are not of personal description or application; for, then, they denote distinct things or qualities: as, Τιμοθεῳ, γνησιῳ τεκνῳ εν πι5ει, χαρις, ελεος, ειρηνη απο Θε8 Πατρος ἡμων, και Χρι58 Ιησ8 τ8 κυρι8 ἡμων. 1 Tim. i. 2. 2 Tim. i. 2. Titus, i. 4.† See also 2 John, 3.

Wetstein's Testimony. Now compare this expression *(εν φοβῳ Χρι58)* with 1 Pet. ii. 17. τον Θεον φοβεισθε, τον βασιλεα τιματε: and also with 2 Kings, xvii. 35 and 36. " *Ye shall not fear*" (rendered by the seventy ου φοβηθησεσθε) " *other gods; but* JEHOVAH, *who brought you out of* " *the land of Egypt, &c. him shall ye fear.*"

* Here the *command of Christ* is mentioned jointly with the command of *God* himself; which is a mode of expression never used concerning any other man, but the *Man Christ Jesus* our Lord, " *by whom are all things:* (1 Cor. viii. 66. Hebrews, i. 2. John, i. 3. Col. 1. 16.) and " *by whom all things consist.*" Col. 1. 17.

† In all these three texts, and in 2 John, 3, there is a manifest supplication made to *Christ, jointly with God the Father,* for *grace, mercy,* and *peace;* all divine gifts. The supplications, therefore, must necessarily be considered as acts of *supreme worship to both.*

3. εςαι μεθ᾽ ὑμων χαρις, ελεΟ᾽, ειρηνη, παρα Θεε Πατρος, και παρα Κυριου Ιησου Χριςε τε ᾽Τιε τε Πατρος, εν αληθεια και αγαπη.

RULE V.

And also when there is no article . before the first noun, the insertion of the copulative και before the next noun, cr name, of the same case, denotes a different person or thing from the first: as in the following examples.* Πασα ΠΙΚΡΙΑ,

και

* Note by the Author. [In the former editions of this little work, as well as in the original MS. of it, the 1ſt verſe of the general epiſtle of St James was cited as the *firſt* example of this 5th rule ; viz. Ιακωβ☉· Θεε και Κυριε Ιησε Χριςε δουλος. For, the author had ſuppoſed that the words Θεε και Κυριε, having no article before the firſt ſubſtantive, muſt here denote two different perſons, according to the general idiom of ſimilar expreſſions throughout the New Teſtament, when the copulative is inſerted without the article; but, having ſince read the juſt reaſons and ample teſtimonies produced for a *contr ᷓᷓ* interpretation of *this particular text,* in one of the *ſix letters* addreſſed to himſelf (p. 114 to 120) by the Rev. Mr *Chr. Wordſworth,* (for, it would be injuſtice to conceal that gentleman's name, ſince his merit and indefatigable labour, in forming that learned work, have been ſo generally approved,) he is thereby convinced that this

text

και ΘΥΜΟΣ, και ΟΡΓΗ, και ΚΡΑΥΓΗ, και ΒΛΑΣ-
ΦΗΜΙΑ, αρθητω αφ' υμων, συν παση κακια, Ephef.
iv. 31. This laſt ſentence contains four examples of the fifth rule. ΧΑΡΙΣ υμιν και ΕΙΡΗΝΗ
απο ΘΕΟΥ ΠΑΤΡΟΣ ημων και ΚΥΡΙΟΥ ΙΗΣΟΥ
ΧΡΙΣΤΟΥ. 2 Cor. i. 2. 1 Ephef. i. 2. Gal. i.
3. Philem. 3. ΕΙΡΗΝΗ τοις αδελφοις ΚΑΙ ΑΓΑΠΗ
μετα πιστεως απο ΘΕΟΥ ΠΑΤΡΟΣ ΚΑΙ ΚΥΡΙΟΥ
ΙΗΣΟΥ ΧΡΙΣΤΟΥ, Ephef. vi. 23.*

C   Except

text may with more propriety be placed among the *exceptions* to the fifth and ſix rules than as an *example* of the
fifth; and he hath, therefore, withdrawn it from the
examples, notwithſtanding that Mr Wordſworth hath
produced (in p. 120) the authority even of an antient
Greek writer for that example, in the ſame ſenſe that was
at firſt cited in this place as denoting two diſtinct perſons,
contrary to Mr Wordſworth's own opinion of it. "But
"there is *one* Greek writer" (ſays he) "who has clearly
"adopted the other interpretation. It is Œcumenius, in
"his commentary. Ιακωβος Θεu και Κυριu Ιησu Χριςu δου-
"λος ταις δωδεκα κ. τ. λ. Θεu μεν τu Πατρος, Κυριu δε τu
"υιu," &c. Vol. ii. p. 441.]

  * The ſupplications for *grace* and *peace* jointly from
God the Father, and from the Lord Jeſus Chriſt, in all
theſe five texts laſt cited, are ſo many unqueſtionable inſtances of *prayer* and *ſupreme worſhip* to CHRIST, as being

                  a

Except the numerical adjective εἷς precedes
the firſt noun; in which caſe the copulative
καὶ will have the ſame effect that it has
between two nouns where only the firſt is
preceded by the article, agreeably to the firſt
rule; as, Εἷς ΘΕΟΣ ΚΑΙ ΠΑΤΗΡ παντων, ὁ επι
παντων, και δια παντων, και εν πασιν ὑμιν. Epheſ.
iv. 6.

RULE VI.

And as the inſertion of the copulative καὶ *between nouns of the ſame caſe,* without articles,
*(according to the fifth rule,) denotes that the
ſecond noun expreſſes a* different perſon, thing,
or quality, from the preceding noun, *ſo, like-
wiſe,* the ſame effect *attends the copulative
when each of the nouns are preceded by articles:*
as in the following examples.—Ὁ νομ☉ δια Μω-
σεως εδοθη· Ἡ χαρις ΚΑΙ Ἡ αληθεια δια Ιησ8 Χρις8
εγενετο, John, i. 17. ὁτε 8ν ηγερθη" (Ιησ8ς) " εκ
νεκρων, εμνησθησαν ὁι μαθηται αυτ8, ὁτι τ8το ελεγεν
αυτοις, και επιςευσαν τῃ γραφῃ, και τῳ λογῳ ῳ
εισπεν

a free diſpoſer of thoſe divine gifts *jointly* with his Almighty Father; agreeably to what I have already remarked
above on 1 Theſſ. iii. 11, and Titus, i. 1.

ειπεν ὁ Ιησυς, John, ii. 22. — φωνη μεγαλη εκραυ-
γασε," (Ιησυς) " Λαζαρε, δευρο εξω. Και εξηλθεν
ὁ τεθνηκως, δεδεμεν☞ ΤΟΥΣ ΠΟΔΑΣ ΚΑΙ ΤΑΣ
ΧΕΙΡΑΣ κειριαις, και ἡ οψις αυτε σουδαριω περιεδεδετο.
John, xi. 44. — εις επιγνωσιν τε μυςηριε ΤΟΥ ΘΕΟΥ
και Πατρ☞, ΚΑΙ ΤΟΥ ΧΡΙΣΤΟΥ, εν ᾡ εισι παντες
ὁι θησαυροι ΤΗΣ ΣΟΦΙΑΣ ΚΑΙ ΤΗΣ ΓΝΩΣΕΩΣ
αποκρυφοι. Col. ii. 2. ὑπομνησιν λαμβανων της εν
σοι ανυποκριτου πιςεως, ἡτις ενῳκησε πρωτον εν τῃ
μαμμη σε Λωϊδι και τῃ μητρι σε Ευνεικῃ· πεπεισμαι
δε, ὁτι και εν σοι, 2 Tim. i. 5. — ἱνα εν πασι δοξαζη-
ται ὁ Θε☞ δια Ιησε Χριςε, ᾡ εςιν Ἡ δοξα ΚΑΙ ΤΟ
κρατ☞ εις τες αιωνας των αιωνων. Αμην. 1 Pet.
iv. 11.

Except diſtinct and different actions are
intended to be attributed to *one and the ſame
perſon*; in which caſe, if the ſentence is not
expreſſed agreeably to the three firſt rules,
but appears as an exception to this ſixth rule,
or even to the fifth, (for, this *exception* relates
to both rules,) the context muſt explain or point
out plainly the perſon to whom the two nouns
relate: as in 1 Theſſ. iii. 6. Αρτι δε ΕΛΘΟΝ-
ΤΟΣ ΤΙΜΟΘΕΟΥ προς ἡμας αφ᾽ ὑμων ΚΑΙ ΕΥΑΓ-
ΓΕΛΙΣΑΜΕΝΟΥ ἡμιν την πιςιν, &c. And alſo in

John,

John, xx. 28. ` Και απεκριθη ο Θωμας, και ειπεν αυτω Ό ΚΥΡΙΟΣ με ΚΑΙ Ό ΘΕΟΣ με. If the two nouns (viz. ο Κυριος and ο Θεϕ) were the leading nominative fubftantives of a fentence, they would exprefs the defcriptive qualities or dignities of *two diftinct perfons*, according to the fixth rule ; but, in this laft text, two diftinct divine characters are applied to *one perfon* only ; for, the context clearly expreffes *to whom the words were addreffed by Thomas:* which perfpicuity *in the addrefs* clearly proves, likewife, the futility of that glofs for which the Arians and Socinians contend; viz. that Thomas could not mean that *Chrift was his God*, but only uttered, in his furprife, a folemn exclamation or ejaculation to God. The text, however, exprefsly relates that our Lord firft addreffed himfelf to Thomas: ειτα λεγει τω Θωμα, φερε τον δακτυλον σε ωδε, &c. και απεκριθη ο Θωμας και ειπεν αυτω, (that is, without doubt, to Jesus,) ο Κυριος μου, και ο Θεϕ με. So that both thefe *diftinct* titles (for, they are plainly mentioned as *diftinct*) were manifeftly addreffed, αυτω, to that *one perfon*, *Jefus*, to whom *Thomas replied*, as the text exprefsly informs us.

The

The language is fo plain, when the whole context is confidered, that the Socinian perverfion of it is notorious. See alfo 1 Cor. i. 24. —— Χριϛον Θεȣ δυναμιν και Θεȣ σοφιαν,* and Acts, ii. 36.† There are alfo other examples of this exception which clearly prove that *Chriſt is God:* as, Μη φοβȣ. ΕΓΩ ειμι Ὁ πρωτος ΚΑΙ Ὁ εσχατ☉, ΚΑΙ Ὁ ΖΩΝ.‡ και εγενομην νεκρος, και ιδȣ ζων ειμι εις τους αιωνας των αιωνων· αμην. Κᾳ εχω τας κλεις τȣ ᾁδȣ και τȣ θανατȣ.‡ Rev. i. 17, 18.

Thefe are the words of him whom John faw, ὁμοιον Ὑιῳ ανθρωπȣ, with a two-edged fword proceeding out of his mouth; which was undoubtedly a reprefentation of the Λογ☉, or word of God, as this declaration alludes plainly to his death and refurrection. Εγενομηυ νεκρος, και ιδȣ ζων ειμι. And again in the fecond

C 3   chapter,

---

* Example of the exception to the fifth rule.

† Note lately added by the Author. [See alfo James, i, i. the text withdrawn from the examples of the fifth rule for the reafons affigned by the learned and Rev. Mr Chr. Wordfworth, in his fix letters to the author, p. 114 to 120.]

‡ Example of the exception to the fixth rule.

chapter, ver. 8. ταδε λεγει Ὁ πρωτος ΚΑΙ Ὁ εσχα-
τ☉,* (and the fame infallible mark of diftinction is added to prove which of the
divine perfons is here to be underftood,)
ΟΣ εγενετο νεκρος, και εζησεν. Now, though the
explanation which Grotius has given us of
thefe titles (ὁ πρωτ☉ και ὁ εσχατ☉) is certainly
true when applied to Chrift, yet it does not
appear to be the *whole truth*, or the full
meaning that ought to be attributed to thefe
titles, either in the Revelation or elfewhere;
for, they have a manifeft reference to the
fupreme titles of *the Almighty* in the firft chapter and eighth verfe, (which alfo contains
examples of this exception,) ΕΓΩ ειμι ΤΟ Α και
ΤΟ Ω,* λεγει Ὁ κυριος, αρχη και τελος,† Ὁ ων ΚΑΙ
Ὁ ην,* και Ὁ ερχομενος, ὁ παντοκρατωρ. And, in
the 22d chapter, 13th verfe, where thefe titles,
το Α και το Ω, are manifeftly, by the context,
to be underftood as the titles of Chrift, we
find them explained by thefe other titles, ὁ
πρωτ☉ και ὁ εσχατος, to which Grotius has attributed a much inferior and lefs comprehen-
                                        five

---

* Example of the exception to the fixth rule.

† Example of the exception to the fifth rule.

five meaning. Εγω ειμι ΤΟ Α ΚΑΙ ΤΟ Ω,* αρχη
και τελος,† Ὁ πρωτος και Ὁ εσχατος.* And
as I have fhewn in my Tract on *the Law* of
Nature, &c. p. 270 and 271, that thefe titles,
" *the firft* and *the laft*," are antient titles of
Jehovah, in the Old Teftament, to declare his
eternal exiftence, there can be no juft reafon for
giving them an inferior fenfe when they are
applied to Chrift, who was truly *Jehovah*, as
a variety of texts demonftrate. [*Law of
Nature*, p. 248 to 345.]

Another example of the exception to the
fifth rule occurs in the Rev. xx. 2. — τον οφιν
τον αρχαιον, ὁς εςι ΔΙΑΒΟΛΟΣ ΚΑΙ ΣΑΤΑΝΑΣ.
Thefe are two different names, or appellatives,
attributed (by the explanatory words ὁς εςι) to
the fame Old Serpent.

THE END OF THE RULES.

The various ufes of the article and copulative, expreffed in the five laft rules and
their exceptions, muft amply illuftrate, to
every

---

* Example of the exception to the fixth rule.
† Example of the exception to the fifth rule.

every attentive reader, the difference and
particularity of thofe fentences which fall
under the firft and principal rule; and therefore I may now proceed with more confidence
to point out feveral important corrections
that ought to be made in our common
tranflation of the New Teftament, if the feveral fentences, which fall under the *firft
rule,* be duly weighed and confidered; —
corrections which may be fairly defended,
I apprehend, by the authority of the feveral
examples from which thofe rules were formed.

EXAMPLES

Of fentences which fall under the FIRST RULE,
*and are improperly rendered in the Englifh
verfion.*

EXAMPLE I. ₂ Pet. i. 1.— εν δικαιοσυνη ΤΟΥ
ΘΕΟΥ ἡμων ΚΑΙ ΣΩΤΗΡΟΣ ἡμων ΙΗΣΟΥ ΧΡΙΣΤΟΥ.
As the article τȣ is not repeated before the
next defcriptive noun, σωτηρος, it is manifeft
that both the nouns are to be referred to
one and the fame perfon; and, therefore, in
order to turn it into an intelligible Englifh
phrafe, the *proper name* to which the *two
defcriptive*

descriptive nouns refer ought to be placed first; as, " By the righteousnefs of Jesus " Chrift, OUR GOD and our SAVIOUR." Among the various readings collected by Curcellæus, it appears that in fome copies the word ήμων was not repeated after σωτηρος, and I have by me twenty different editions (including thofe of Erafmus, Stephens, Dr Mill, Bengelius, &c.) which follow that reading; viz. εν δικαιοσυνη ΤΟΥ ΘΕΟΥ ήμων ΚΑΙ σωτηρος Ιησυ Χριςυ, in which cafe, a literal ren- dering into Englifh will fufficiently exprefs the fenfe of the Greek without tranfpofing the *proper name*; viz. " *Through the righteouf-* " *nefs of our God and Saviour, Jefus Chrift.*" The fenfe and purport, however, is exactly the fame in both the readings; and, in the old Englifh editions, has generally been ex- preffed in the terms required by my firft rule; viz. " *In the righteoufnefs that cometh of* " *oure God and Saviour, Jefu Chrift.*" (fol. edit. 1549.) — " *Through the righteoufneffe of* " *our God and Saviour, Jefus Chrift.*" (12mo edit. 1595.) — " *By the righteoufneffe of our* " *God and Saviour, Jefus Chrift.*" (4to edit. 1599.)

1599.) — "*The righteousness of Jesus Christ,*
"*our God and Saviour.*" (margin of the fo-
lio edit. 1611.) And even in the margin
of our prefent verfion the proper reading is
"*of our God and Saviour,*" manifeftly referring both titles to one perfon. The learned
Beza alfo remarks, on the words of this
text, "*Ista necesse est conjunctim legamus quia*
"*unicus est articulus, ut copiosius diximus* Tit.
"*ii. 13. Itaque continet etiam hic locus mani-*
"*festum divinitatis Christi testimonium.*" The
two nouns are referred to Chrift alfo in the
Syriac verfion. There feems, therefore, to
be ample authority for my firft rule.

Exam. II. Titus, ii. 13. — επιφανειαν της δοξης
ΤΟΥ μεγαλ8 Θε8 ΚΑΙ σωτηρος ημων Ιησ8 Χρις8.
In fome few copies a comma is inferted between Θε8 and και, but without authority.
The above-mentioned note of Beza, upon this
text, is too long to be inferted here at length,
and therefore I muft refer you to the author
himfelf. He infifts, however, that thefe two
titles do not refer to two diftinct perfons,
becaufe the article is omitted before the fecond. In the prefent Englifh verfion it is
rendered

rendered — " *the glorious appearing of the great*
" *God and our Saviour Jesus Christ:*" but
so great is the difference between the idiom
of the Greek tongue and that of the English,
that a *literal translation* will not always
express the same sense without some little
transposition in the order of the words; and,
therefore, though the pronoun ἡμων is placed
after the two descriptive nouns that are applicable only to *one* person as they are expressed
in *the Greek*, yet the rendering of the said
pronoun *in English* ought to be PREFIXED
to the said descriptive nouns, in order to express the *same sense* in a proper English
phrase; as, — " *the glorious appearing of* OUR
" *great God and Saviour, Jesus Christ.*" —
This is the rendering of the learned Hugh
Broughton, according to a printed English
Bible, corrected *with a pen*, in my collection.
It might, indeed, be *literally* rendered without transposition of the pronoun; viz. " *the*
" *great God and Saviour* OF US," instead of
" OUR *great God and Saviour:*" but the latter is more agreeable to the general mode of
expressing that pronoun in English. Thus
Christ

Chrift is not only entitled *God*, but even the
" *great God*," according to the plaineft grammatical conftruction of the text: and, indeed,
if we duly weigh the evidence of his
being really *Jehovah*, and *one with the Father*,
[εγω και ὁ Πατηρ ἑν εσμεν, the plural verb
εσμεν (" *we are*") marking the plurality, or
diftinction of more perfons than one, as
much as the noun ἑν marks the *unity* of their
exiftence,] he muft neceffarily be efteemed
" *the great God*,"* becaufe there is but ONE
GOD.

G. S.

* As we believe that three perfons exift in one and the
fame God, we cannot believe any one of them to be lefs
than God, without denying the unity of the Godhead. And,
as each perfon is God, it follows that each muft be *the great
God*. Theophylact bears an explicit teftimony to this conclufion in his commentary on St Paul's epiftle to Titus, ii.
13. " Που δε εισιν (fays the learned and venerable commen-
tator, exultingly, on the authority of this paffage of Titus)
" που δε εισιν ὁι τον υιον ἐλαττουντες, και ουδε Θεον ανεχομενοι
λεγειν; Ακουσιλοσαν, ὁτι και ΘΕΟΣ εστι, και ΜΕΓΑΣ.
Το δε μεγας επι Θεου λεγεται, ου κατα συγκρισιν την προς
αλλον μικρον, αλλ᾽ απολελυμενως, ὡς φυσει ΑΥΤΟΜΕΓΑΛΟΥ
οντος:" *Now what becomes of their objections, who degrade the
dignity of the Son, not allowing him even the name of God? Let
them*

them learn, from this paffage, that he is not only God but our great
God. *He is called* great God, *not relatively, by comparifon with
another inferior God, but, abfolutely, from his own native and
effential greatnefs.* Whitby, in his note on the fame paffage
of Titus, has given fome very folid reafons for applying the
terms μεγαλου Θεου to our Saviour. His words are:
" Here it deferveth to be noted, that it is highly probable,
" that Jefus Chrift is here ftyled *the great God;* firft, be-
" caufe in the original the article is prefixed only before
" the *great God,* and therefore feems to require this con-
" ftruction, ' the appearance of Jefus Chrift the great God
" ' and our Saviour.' Secondly, becaufe as God the Fa-
" ther is not faid properly to *appear,* fo the word επιφα-
" νεια never occurs in the New Teftament, but when it is
" applied to Jefus Chrift, and fome coming of his; the
" places, in which it is to be found, being only thefe, 2
" Theff. ii. 8. 1 Tim. vi. 14. 2 Tim. i. 10. and iv. 1,
" 8. Thirdly, becaufe Chrift is emphatically ftyled
" *our hope, the hope of* our glory. Col. i. 27. 1 Tim. i. 1.
" And, laftly, becaufe not only all the antient commenta-
" tors on the place do fo interpret this text, but the Ante-
" Nicene fathers alfo; Hippolytus (Antichrift. fect. 64)
" fpeaking of ' the appearance of our God and Saviour Je-
" fus Chrift;' and Clemens of Alexandria (ad Gent. p.
" 5, 6) proving Chrift to be both God and Man, our
" Creator, and the author of all our good things, from
" thefe very words of St Paul." *Vid. tract. de vera Chrifti
dettate,* p. 44, 45. Hammond, alfo, in his literal mar-
ginal verfion, tranflates επιφανειαν της δοξης του μεγαλου Θεου

και

καὶ σωτηρος ἡμων Ιησου Χριςου, thus, "the appearance of "the glory of our great God and Saviour Jesus Christ."

EDITOR.

The remainder of this letter is lost. The author had not leisure to copy the original letter before he sent it to the gentleman to whom it was addressed, and therefore he requested him to return it as soon as he had perused and considered it; but the gentleman neglected this request; and the author, after several years solicitation, obtained only a part of the letter, (as far as is here copied,) and the remainder (which was written on a separate half-sheet) he has never yet been able to recover. He had however a short memorandum of the several texts, which were explained in the latter part of the letter; and, having since had favourable opportunities of examining the said texts, and of copying them very accurately from the antient Alexandrian manuscript in the British Museum, he has been enabled to make some short remarks on the versions of all the said texts, which may serve as a sufficient Supplement to this imperfect letter. Some notes have been added to this printed copy which were not in the original letter.

G. S.

EXAMPLES

EXAMPLE I.

ACTS, XX. 28.

ΠΡΟΣΕΧΕΤΕ ουν ἑαυτοις και παντι τῳ ποιμνιῳ εν ᾡ ὑμας το πνευμα το ἁγιον εθετο επισκοπους ποιμαιν-ειν την εκκλησιαν τȣ Θεȣ, ἡν περιεποιησατο δια τȣ ιδιȣ αἱματος.

The warning of the apostle Paul to the presbyters of the church of Ephesus, which is thus rendered in the common English version: " Take heed therefore unto yourselves, " and to all the flock over which the *holy* " *Ghost* hath made you overseers, to feed " the church of *God*, which he hath purchased " with his own blood."

In

In the Alexandrian MS. and a few other
MSS. inſtead of τȣ Θεȣ, which is the moſt
general reading, the word Κυριȣ is ſubſtituted;
but many old MSS. have both words, τȣ
Κυριȣ και Θεȣ,* whereby the text is brought
within the conſtruction of the 1ſt rule, and
ſhould be rendered, — " To feed the church
" of the *Lord, even of God*, which he hath
" purchaſed with *his own blood*."

Though there is no word in the Greek to
correſpond with this word " *even*," ſo as that
it might be deemed a *literal rendering*, yet
this Engliſh word is frequently uſed by our
tranſlators to expreſs the *identity of perſon*,
when a copulative, in the Greek text, joins
a ſecond ſubſtantive (i. e. of *perſonal* deſcription without an article) to the former ſubſtantive, preceded by an article, agreeably
to

---

* Note lately added by the Author. [Three of the
antient Greek MSS. in the Cæſarian Library at Vienna,
and 1 Sclavonian MS. (cited in the Vienna edition of
1787,) have this reading; and it is inſerted in the margin
of the elegant 12mo edition of 1553, printed by John
Criſpin. For the ſame reading Dr Mill refers to fifteen
MSS.]

to the firſt rule; as in Romans, xv. 6. τον Θεον
και Πατερα, and I. Cor. xv. 24. τῳ Θεῳ και
Πατρι: both of which are rendered, — " *God,*
" *even the Father,* (inſtead of the literal
rendering, *the God and Father,*) that the
identity of perſon may be the more obvious.
See alſo II. Cor. i. 3: ευλογητος Ὁ ΘΕΟΣ ΚΑΙ
ΠΑΤΗΡ τ8 Κυρι8 ἡμων Ιησ8 Χριϛ8, Ὁ ΠΑΤΗΡ των
οικτιρμων, ΚΑΙ ΘΕΟΣ πασης παρακλησεως. This
ſentence contains two ſucceſſive examples of
the firſt rule, and is rendered, " Bleſſed be
" God, *even* the father of our Lord Jeſus
" Chriſt, the father of mercies, and the God
" of all comfort." See alſo James, iii. 9; τον
Θεον και Πατερα. I. Theſſ. iii. 13; τ8 Θε8 και
Πατρος ἡμων. II. Theſſ. ii. 16; και ὁ Θεος και
Πατηρ. Beſides theſe ſix examples, wherein
the word *even,* in the Engliſh verſion, expreſſes the copulative, there are alſo 13* *other
examples of the firſt rule* in the New Teſtament:
i. e. altogether 19 examples reſpecting our

heavenly

---

* Viz. II. Cor. xi. 31. Gal. i. 4. Epheſ. i. 3, and
iv. 6, and v. 20. Philip, iv. 20. Col. i. 3, and ii. 2,
and iii. 17. I. Theſſ. i. 3, and iii. 11. James, i. 27.
I. Peter, i. 3.

heavenly Father alone; and therefore the 9
examples of the fame mode of expreffion, produced in this and the following pages, refpecting the *fon and the holy fpirit*, ought certainly
to be rendered in a *fenfe* fuitable to the fame
uniform rule of conftruction, to exprefs *the
identity of perfons*, becaufe the fame mode of
grammatical expreffion is ufed in them all.

EXAMPLE II.

EPHESIANS, V. 5.

——*ɛϰ ɛχɛɩ ϰληϱονομιαν ɛν τη βασιλɛıᾳ* ΤΟΥ
ΧΡΙΣΤΟΥ ΚΑΙ ΘΕΟΥ.

In the common Englifh verfion the fentence is rendered, " *No whoremonger,* &c.
" *hath any inheritance in the kingdom of Chrift,*
" *and of God.*" As if two perfons had been
mentioned in the original text ; but, as the
part of the fentence above cited is the ge-
nerally-approved reading of the printed
Greek copies, and as this reading is confirmed
by the Alexandrian MS. and by all other
Greek MSS. of known authority, it affords
an unqueftionable proof againft *the apoftacy*
of

of the Socinians in their *denial of divine honour to our Lord the Chrift, or Meffiah,* who, according to the idiom of the Greek tongue, is in this text exprefsly intitled Θεος, " God," though the proof does not appear in the Englifh verfion. Let it be remarked that the two fubftantives of perfonal defcription, Χρισα and Θεα, are joined by the copulative και, and that the article τα precedes the firft, and that there is no article before the word Θεα, whereby, according to *the firft rule,* both titles are *neceffarily* to be applied to *one* and the fame perfon, and (if literally rendered in Englifh) fhould be, — " hath no " inheritance in the kingdom of *the Chrift* " *and God.*" But this *literal* rendering does not fufficiently exprefs the neceffary doctrine of the Greek, that the *Chrift* is *alfo God:* and therefore to help the Englifh idiom, and to accommodate the rendering more ftrictly to the true meaning of the Greek, the name of *Jefus,* which is neceffary to be *underftood,* might very fairly be inferted in *italic,* or between hooks, as a parenthefis, to fupply the neceffary fenfe of the Greek; as, " in the kingdom
" of

" of (Jefus) the Chrift and God:" or elfe to
be rendered, " *in the kingdom of Chrift, (even)*
" *of God*," as recommended in the firft
example.

EXAMPLE III.

PHILIPIANS, iii. 3.

ἡμεις γαρ εσμεν ἡ περιτονη, ΌΙ πνευματι Θεβ ΛΑ-
ΤΡΕΎΟΝΤΕΣ, ΚΑΙ ΚΑΎΧΩΜΕΝΟΙ εν Χριϛῳ Ιησου,
και ουκ εν σαρκι πεποιϑοτες.

This is rendered, in our common verfion,
— " For we are the circumcifion, which
" worfhip *God* IN the fpirit, and rejoice in
" Chrift Jefus, and have no confidence in
" the flefh."

In the London Polyglott, and many other
valuable editions, the reading is ὁι πνευματι Θεῳ,
but in the Alexandrian MS.* it is ὁι πνευματι Θεβ,
which feems to be the true reading; becaufe
the other is fo unufual an expreffion, that
the generality of tranflators have forced

a

* Note lately added by the Author. [And in the
Vienna edition of 1786, and in all the feven Greek MSS.
of the Imperial Library, that have been feparately collated with it.]

a conſtruction which the context itſelf cannot fairly bear, even if the dative caſe, Θεῳ,
were admitted to be the true reading, unleſs
another word, the prepoſition ɛν, be alſo added
to it before πνευματι, as in John, iv. 23, and
Rom. viii. 9, where the ſenſe, which they
have applied to this text, was really intended:
but, without this addition, (as we may fairly
judge by thoſe examples,) the literal rendering ought to be, " We are the circumciſion,
" who worſhip the ſpirit God." Whereas
they have commonly rendered it as if the
prepoſition ɛν was really inſerted in this text
before the dative, πνευματι, as in the two examples before cited ; viz. " Qui ſpiritu ſervi-
" mus Deo," or " Qui ſpiritu colimus Deum:"
or, as in the Syriac verſion, " Qui Deo ſervi-
" mus in ſpiritu:" (ſyr.) or, as in the common Engliſh verſion, " Which worſhip God
" in the ſpirit." But there is no ſuch prepoſition in the Greek. The difficulty therefore of rendering the common reading, (Θεῳ,)
without ſuppoſing this addition of EN to be
underſtood before πνευματι, proves that the
reading of the Alexandrian MS, in this text

is really to be preferred; οἱ πνευματι ΘΕΟΥ*
λατρευοντες, " *who worſhip the ſpirit of God,*"
whereby the apoſtle and Timothy, as an example to the church at Philippi, aſſert their
profeſſion, that they pay *divine honour to the
ſpirit of God,* and *that they glory in Chriſt.*

EXAMPLE IV.

II. THESS. i. 12.

Κατα την χαριν ΤΟΥ ΘΕΟΥ ἡμων ΚΑΙ ΚΥΡΙΟΥ
Ιησυ Χριςυ.

This, in the common Engliſh verſion, is
rendered (very erroneouſly) as if two diftinct

---

* Many other antient and valuable Greek MSS. as Dr
Mill has teſtified, have this reading, Θευ, but Auguſtine
teſtified, that, in his time, *all* or *almoſt all Greek copies,*
and many Latin, had the reading " SPIRITUI DEI."
" *Plures enim Codices etiam Latini ſic habent, qui* SPIRITUI
" DEI *ſervimus,* GRÆCI *autem* OMNES, AUT PENE
" OMNES. *In nonnullis autem exemplaribus* LATINIS
" *invenimus* non SPIRITUI DEI ſervimus," *ſed*
" SPIRITUI DEO SERVIMUS. *Sed qui in hoc erravit et*
" *authoritati graviori cedere detrectavit,* &*c.*"

In Wetſtein's edition the word Θευ is ſubjoined with
this mark ∞, to denote the *preferable reading.*

tinct perfons were mentioned, viz. " *according*
" *to the grace of our God and the Lord Jefus*
" *Chrift.*" But, if two diftinct perfons had
really been intended to be expreffed, as (by
innumerable examples of the grammatical
conftruction of fentences, for the accurate
diftinction of perfons peculiar to the Greek
tongue, ufed in the Greek Teftament, from
which the preceding rules were formed)
may be demonftrated, the article would
have been repeated (according to the fixth
rule) after the copulative and before the
fecond fubftantive κυριs. For, it is manifeft,
that the infertion of the comma, in fome
Greek copies, after ημων, is a modern
interpolation; becaufe the expedient of
breaking fentences into fmall divifions or
particles by commas, to preferve the neceffary
diftinctions, was not antiently ufed (nor
likely to have been ufed) by the antient
writers of the Greek tongue, who were ac-
cuftomed to much more accurate diftinctions
in their various peculiar modes of grammatical expreffion, fpecified in the fix preceding
rules.

Whole

Whole fentences are, indeed, diftinguifhed, in the oldeft Greek MSS. by a fingle point placed at their end, fometimes towards the top of the line, fometimes in the middle, and fometimes towards the bottom; but, apparently, no diftinction of *time* has been intended by any of thefe three different modes of placing the point, for, they are all placed, indifcriminately, to the moft obvious and full termination of fentences; and, therefore, we may be affured, that, in all thefe three different modes of placing them, they were originally intended only as *periods* to conclude the fentences: fo that, when we find them in the place of commas, to diftinguifh merely the parts or particles of a fentence, there is great reafon to fufpect that they have been the additions of later times.

In the Alexandrian MS. the text before us is awkwardly divided by one of thefe points, placed after the word ἡμων, which point, for the reafon before given, muft neceffarily be deemed a *period*, and which did not exift in the original text of the facred penman.

The

The intention of the tranfcriber, or interpolator, by adding this point to the text, (for
it cannot juftly be attributed to the original
writer,) has been probably to make a diftinction of perfons; as if *two* perfons had been
named in the text inftead of *one*, in like
manner as the comma is added after the
word *God*, in the Englifh verfion, *without
any authority.*

But the neceffary grammatical conftruction
of the whole fentence taken together detects
the interpolator, and demonftrates the abfurd-
ity of fuppofing that any fuch point ever
exifted in the original text, becaufe the words,
which are fevered by the fuppofititious period,
cannot form a grammatical fentence (according
to the ordinary modes of expreffion ufed in the
Greek tongue) by themfelves alone; fo that
the obvious fenfe of the context demonftrates
their neceffary connexion with the preceding
words *in one entire fentence:* and demonftrates,
alfo, at the fame time, the ignorance and
fallacy of the interpolator, who attempted to
make two fentences of it by inferting a full
period.

E

If

If literally rendered, it ought to be, — " *ac-* " *cording to the grace of the God and Lord of* " *us, Jesus Christ:*" but, more in the idiom of our own language, it might be justly rendered, " *according to the grace of Jesus Christ,* " *our God and Lord.*" In either way the neceffary doctrine of *our Lord's divine nature,* manifeftly intended to be expreffed in the original, is duly retained in the propofed verfion.

EXAMPLE V.

I. TIM. V. 21.

Διαμαρτυρομαι ενωπιον ΤΟΥ ΘΕΟΥ ΚΑΙ ΚΥΡΙΟΥ ΙΗΣΟΥ ΧΡΙΣΤΟΥ και των εκλεκτων αγγελων, ινα ταυτα φυλαξης, &c.

This, in the common Englifh verfion, is rendered, — " I charge (thee) before God, and " the Lord Jefus Chrift, and the elect angels, " that thou obferve thefe things, &c."

The word Κυριε* is omitted in the Alexandrian MS. where the reading is ενωπιον του Θεε
και

---

* Note lately added by the Author. [The *Author* acknowledges himfelf to be under great obligation to a
judicious

καὶ Χριςὰ Ἰησὰ. And, as no points are inferted
between the fubftantives, we have the teftimo-

ny

judicious and learned writer in the *Britiſh Critic* for a
very important correction of what was written under this
fifth example, and alfo under the 6th, in the former
editions of this little book; as well as for his general
candour in reviewing, and declaring a decided favourable
opinion upon, the whole defign of it. (See the Britiſh
Critic for July, 1802; and alfo Remarks on a former
edition of the year 1798, in the 15th vol. of the Britiſh
Critic, p. 70.)

Under this fifth example the *Author* had inadvertently
inferted the word Χριςὰ inftead of Κυριὰ, in his report
refpecting the omiffion of a word in the Alexandrian MS.
And, in his remarks on the fixth example, he had reverfed
this miftake by mentioning Κυριὰ inftead of Κριςὰ. As
foon as the Author had read, in the *Britiſh Critic*, the
detection of thefe two errors, he immediately referred to
the original paper on which he at firft, many years ago,
had carefully delineated the feveral texts in queftion from
the Alexandrian MS. in the exact form of the letters and
length of the lines; and, finding therein the true reading
of the MS. as ftated in the *Britiſh Critic*, he was the
more furprized to obferve that *be himſelf* had inadvertently tranfpofed (in his fubfequent remarks drawn from that
very fame paper) the word Χριςὰ for Κυριὰ, and Κυριὰ for
Χριςὰ!

Thefe

ny even of this MS. for a clear declaration
that *Jesus* is *God* as well as *Christ:* and, after
the

Thefe were involuntary errors of the *Author himself*
alone, for which the very worthy and learned *Editor* (who
relied on the *Author's* examination of the MS.) is not at
all refponfible: and the *Author* himself, though he had fo
accurate a delineation of the texts, from the MS. in his
poffeffion, did not obferve this unaccountable tranfpofition
that he had made of the two words, in his remarks, until
he was apprifed of the miftake by the learned writer in
the *Britifh Critic,* for which he thinks himfelf under very
great obligation.   G. S.

An extract from the Britifh Critic is inferted in the
Appendix, not only for the better illuftration of the fubject in queftion, but, alfo, more particularly, to fet forth,
in terms more fatisfactory to the *Author* than any expreffions he himfelf could fuggeft, the indefatigable
labour, learning, and judicious criticifm, of the Rev.
Mr *Chr. Wordfworth,* of Trinity-College, Cambridge, in
his fix letters to G. S. on the fubject of this book; by
which the doctrine, particularly of the *firft rule,* has been
fo amply confirmed.

For the fame reafons are added extracts alfo from the
ingenious and learned obfervations on both thefe works,
(the Remarks by G. S. and Mr Wordfworth's fix letters
to him upon them,) which were publifhed in the *Chriftian
Obferver* for July, 1802, and in the *Chriftian Guardian* for
December, 1802, and alfo in the *Orthodox Churchman's
Magazine and Review* for February, 1803.]

the next copulative, which connects the mention of different perfons, according to the
fixth rule, the adverb ενωπιον, *(before,)* though
not exprefsly repeated, is plainly to be underftood; as, — " *I charge*" (thee), " *before the*
" God *and* Christ, *Jefus,*" (or, rather, *be-*
fore Jefus, the God and Chrift,) " and" (before) " *the elect angels, that thou obferve thefe*
" *things.*" Thus far the teftimony of the Alexandrian MS. — But, according to the com-
monly-received text of the Greek, it ought
to be rendered, in the Englifh idiom, " *I*
" *charge* (thee), *before Jefus Chrift, the* God
" *and* Lord, *and* (before) *the elect angels,*
" *&c.*"

EXAMPLE VI.

II. TIM. iv. 1.

Διαμαρτυρομαι ουν εγω ενωπιον ΤΟΥ ΘΕΟΥ ΚΑΙ
ΚΥΡΙΟΥ ΙΗΣΟΥ ΧΡΙΣΤΟΥ *τ8 μελλοντος κρινειν*
ζωντας και νεκρ8ς, &c. *(Geneva Edit.* 1620.)

In the common Englifh verfion this is rendered, " I charge (thee) therefore before
" God, and the Lord Jefus Chrift, who fhall
" judge the quick and the dead &c."

In

In the Greek of this text, as it is commonly printed, the article τ8 is repeated before
Κυρι8, which, fo far, affords an excufe for the
prefent Englifh verfion in placing the comma
after the word *God*, to denote *two* diftinct perfons, according to the fixth rule; but, in the
Alexandrian MS. and feveral other old copies,
*[where the reading is ενωπιον τ8 Θε8 · και Χριϛ8
Ιησ8] the article τ8 is *not* repeated after the
copulative before Χριϛ8: fo that the expreffion
is fimilar, in effect, to the declaration of our
Lord's *divine nature*, by the fame apoftle, in
the preceding example, viz. I. Tim. v. 21.
In fome printed editions the word Κυρι8 is alfo
omitted, but, in the Geneva edition of 1620,
with Scaliger's notes, the word Κυρι8 is inferted
and the article τ8 omitted,† whereby the title

Θε8,

* [·] Correction and addition by the Author.

† Note lately added by the Author. [The expreffion
being exactly the fame as that which is generally allowed
to exift in the preceding example, viz. ενωπιον τ8 Θε8 και
Κυρι8 Ιησ8 Χριϛ8, I. Tim. v. 21. And the Author has
lately difcovered feveral other editions of the Greek
Teftament which have this reading, and thereby confirm
the

Θεʊ, (God,) muſt neceſſarily be conſtrued in
ſuch a manner that it may be clearly underſtood,

the truth of this 6th example; though it muſt be allowed,
at the ſame time, that *not even one* of the ſeveral *editors*
underſtood the text in its proper *grammatical ſenſe*, becauſe
they have all (without any authority) placed commas after
Θεʊ, in order to diſtinguiſh *two perſons*, contrary to the
neceſſary grammatical conſtruction of the Greek text.
Two of theſe editions (in the Author's poſſeſſion) have
Montanus's interlineary Latin verſion. They are both in
8vo, though of different ſizes, the one having four more
lines in each page than the other; but the title-pages of
both being loſt their reſpective dates cannot be known.
(There are ſeveral other 8vo editions with the ſame interlineary verſion, but which have a *different* reading in this
place, viz. the common reading with the article inſerted
in the ſecond place after the copulative; and two ſuch
editions are alſo in the Author's collection.) The fourth
printed authority, which the Author has found, in favour
of his ſixth example, is the Vienna edition of 1787,
printed from an antient MS. in the Imperial Library at
Vienna. The title of it is, " *Novum Teſtamentum ad*
" *Codicem Vindebonenſem Græcè expreſſum. Varietatem*
" *Lectionis addidit Franciſcus Carolus Alter Profeſſor*
" *Gymnaſii Vindebonenſis.*" At the end of the ſecond
volume (for it conſiſts of two very thick 8vo volumes) are
added the various readings of ſeven other antient Greek
MSS.

ftood, in all verfions, to be expreffly applied
to *Chrift*, as it really is in the original. The
tranfcriber

MSS. all containing the Epiftles, (befides the MS. from
which the edition was formed,) which have been feparately collated with this edition; and the variations are
diftinctly and feparately ftated, under the proper titles of
each MS. in the Appendix. Two, only, of all thefe
eight MSS. have, in this text, the article τȣ repeated
in the fecond place after the copulative, (viz. τȣ Θιȣ και
τȣ Κυριȣ, &c.) Another of them has the fame reading
exactly as the Alexandrian MS. τȣ Θιȣ και Χριϛȣ Ιησȣ:
and, therefore, by the omiffion of the article in the
fecond place before Χριϛȣ, doth alfo, equally with that
MS. confirm the doctrine of my fixth example. And all
the other five MSS. (which likewife contain this Epiftle)
muft neceffarily be allowed to have the other more correct
reading for which I contend, viz. τȣ Θιȣ και Κυριȣ Ιησȣ
Χριϛȣ: becaufe no difference or variation from that
reading, in the printed edition, is noted in any other of
the feven feparate collations of antient MSS. that have
been diftinctly compared with it, except in the three that
are firft mentioned above.

Though the infertion of the article in the fecond place
is undoubtedly the moft common reading in all the printed
editions, (for fifty-nine out of fixty-four printed Greek
Teftaments, in the poffeffion of the Author of this little
work, have this reading,) yet feveral of the moft learned
Editors

tranfcriber or interpolator of the Alexandrian
MS. however, being aware of this doctrine,
has

Editors of thefe fifty-nine editions, that have adopted it,
have, at the fame time, warned us that there are various
readings in this text, viz. Bifhop *Walton, Curcellæus,*
Bifhop *Fell,* Dr *Mill, Henry Wetften,* and *John Jac.
Wetften.* The latter cites no lefs than fix antient MSS.
(befides feveral verfions,) which have *not* the reading τȣ
Κυριȣ. (N.B. His mark for a deficiency is a fhort line,
thus — ; and he has expreffed this various reading, in his
note on the text, as follows: " τȣ Κυριȣ.] — A C D a
" prima manu. F G. 31. *Editio Vulg. Copt. Æthiop. Ba-*
" *filius* Eth. 89. *Hilarius.*") And confequently we muft
underftand that all thefe fix MSS. have the fame reading
as the firft of them, A, by which mark he refers to the
Alexandrian MS. wherein, though the words τȣ Κυριȣ are
indeed omitted, yet the proper effect of this omiffion
ought to be at the fame time remarked, viz. that the
article τȣ is not repeated after the copulative, in the
fecond place, before the next noun Χριτȣ: fo that the
expreffion, in all thefe fix MSS. muft be equally declara-
tory of our Lord's divine nature, as in the former example
(the fifth) from I. Tim. v. 21. To the evidence of thefe
fix MSS. muft be added that of *one* of the Imperial MSS.
at *Vienna,* mentioned above.

John Jac. Wetften (my authority for the evidence of
five of the antient MSS. which agree with the Alexandrian
MS.

has endeavoured to pervert it by adding a full period after the word Θεε, as Θυ· But this

period

MS. in the particular reading of the text laſt-mentioned) has alſo acknowleged a very conſiderable degree of evidence in favour of the other reading, which I have adopted as my ſixth example; (though he was, apparently, of a very different opinion from myſelf reſpecting the propriety of it;) for, he cites no leſs than three MSS. (beſides the Geneva edition, which I have quoted) wherein the reading, as he aſſerts, *is without the article in the ſecond place*. See his note, vol. ii, p. 364, viz. " τυ ſecundo " loco.] — E. 4. 52. Editio *Genev.* The ſhort line — is his mark, or ſign, for a deficiency, as ſignified in his prolegomena, p. 221; (laſt line but one;) viz. " — in V. " L." (i. e. in Variis Lectionibus,) "*notat voces, quibus* " *appoſitum eſt, in codd. citatis non legi.*" And E is his mark for the antient *Baſil* MS. But he muſt have made ſome miſtake reſpecting the two otner MSS. 4 and 52, for he has deſcribed them in his prolegomena (p. 46 and 51) as containing the *four Goſpels,* without making any mention of their having alſo the *Epiſtles;* ſo that theſe two MSS. have probably been cited, by miſtake, inſtead of ſome other MSS. which he had known to contain the ſame reading as the *Baſil* MS. and the *Geneva* Edition.

But, even if we ſet aſide theſe two ſuppoſed MSS. yet as it appears that five out of the eight antient MSS. in the Imperial Library at *Vienna,* as well as the antient *Baſil* MS.

period is unqueſtionably ſuppoſititious, becauſe the words before and after the period are *not two diſtinct ſentences,* but obviouſly portions only of *one entire ſentence,* which muſt neceſſarily be conſtrued together, according to the ordinary rules of expreſſion in the Greek tongue, as I have remarked on a preceding example; whereby a ſecond ſubſtantive of perſonal deſcription, *without an article before it,* joined by a copulative to a preceding ſubſtantive of the like nature, and in the ſame caſe, *with an article before it,* muſt neceſſarily denote a farther deſcription of the ſame perſon, expreſſed by the firſt ſubſtantive; (whenever there is an article before the firſt ſubſtantive and none before the ſecond;) ſo that the inſertion of the *period* in the Alexan-

drian

MS. cited by Wetſten, and alſo four printed editions, have this reading; and that ſix other MSS. agree with the Alexandrian MS. in a different reading of this text, which bears equal teſtimony to *the divinity of Chriſt;* the Author hopes it will be allowed that all this united evidence affords ſome reaſonable ground of juſtification for his having cited this text as his ſixth example.]

drian MS.* after Θεκ is utterly vain, becaufe the *copulative* fuÍiciently proves the *connection* of the two fubftantives in one clear fentence, and the omiffion of the article before the fecond fubftantive induces the neceffity of applying the fame grammatical conftruction, whereby alone the due diftinction of perfons is fo peculiarly maintained in the Greek tongue, and *not by points*. The text fhould therefore be rendered, — " I charge (thee,) therefore, " before the God and Lord, Jefus Chrift, &c." Or, rather, (to render the doctrine more obvious in the Englifh idiom,) — " I charge " (thee,) therefore, before Jefus Chrift, the " God and Lord, who fhall judge the quick " and the dead, &c." And thus the texts in the two laft examples will perfectly accord as the uniform expreffions of the fame apoftle, afferting,

---

* Note lately added by the Author. [And alfo the infertion of commas after Θικ, in the four printed editions, is equally vain, and proves only that the Editors were not aware of the proper grammatical conftruction of the text.]

afferting, in both,* the *divinity of his Lord and Saviour*, by whom he had been perfonally fummoned to bear his teftimony to the gentiles, as being an eye and ear witnefs of his *glorious majefty*.

Our Socinian Sadducees, who have impioufly entitled our Lord " *a mere man*," and " *nothing but a man*," and " *fimple human na-* " *ture*," will not be able to digeft this neceffary doctrine until they humble themfelves to receive inftructions from the holy fcriptures.

F   EXAMPLE

---

* Note lately added by the Author. [This feems to have been the opinion alfo of the learned *Bengelius*, that both thefe texts had originally the fame mode of expreffion. For, in his Gnomon, he remarks, on the text of the former example, (1 Tim. v. 21,) και Κυρια et Domini, " Articulus non additur, cum tamen mox adda- " tur de angelis. Ergo *Dei* appellatio et *Domini* ad unum " pertinet fubjectum. Conf. tamen II. Tim. iv. 1, κυρια " non habet lectio vetufta." To reftore this *antient reading without the article in the fecond place*, there feems to be ample authority by the teftimony of the MSS. and editions which I have cited, in addition to *the fimilarity of expreffion*, by the *fame apoftle*, in I. Tim. v. 21.]

EXAMPLE VII.

TIT. ii. 13.

—— Προσδεχομενοι την μακαριαν ελπιδα και
επιφανειαν της δοξης ΤΟΥ μεγαλε ΘΕΟΥ ΚΑΙ
ΣΩΤΗΡΟΣ ἡμων ΙΗΣΟΥ ΧΡΙΣΤΟΥ.

The prefent verfion of thefe words, in
the Englifh teftament, is, —— " Looking for
" that bleffed hope, and the glorious appearing
" of the great God, and our Saviour Jefus
" Chrift." This text (though the next in
order, according to the ufual mode of arran-
ging the books of the New Teftament) has
already been produced as the fecond example
in the preceding letter. I have fince, however,
examined the Alexandrian MS. and find that
it agrees exactly with the above citation of this
text, except that a point has been added in the
MS. after the word Θεε or Θυ. On which it
is neceffary to obferve, that the fame remarks
are obvioufly applicable to this fuperfluous and
abfurd addition of the point or *period*, that I
have made on the texts II. Theff. i. 12, and
II. Tim. iv. 1, in the fourth and fixth examples

ples of this tract. For, as the proper effect
or purpose of *periods* is to separate words
into *distinct sentences*, it is obvious that the
words, which follow the suppositicious period
in this text, are incapable of a grammatical
construction without reference to the preceding
words connected by the *copulative*: and therefore the *note of separation* (a period) cannot
possibly have been intended by the inspired
writer. This testimony, therefore, of the
sacred text, in favour of our Lord's *divine
nature*, ought not to be withheld from the
mere English reader.

I am persuaded that our modern Socinians
would not have made so much clamour,
about *the necessity of a new translation*, had
they been aware that a more close and literal
rendering of the original text (even in passages
which had escaped their calumnious charges of
corruption, and their arrogant attempts at
imaginary *correction*) must necessarily cut up
their favourite system by the roots.

The text in question, if the truth of the
original be duly regarded, must inevitably be
rendered, " *Expecting the blessed hope and ap-*

" *pearance*

" *pearance of the glory of our great God and*
" *Saviour, Jesus Christ.*"

EXAMPLE VIII.

II. PET. i. i.

— εν δικαιοσυνη ΤΟΥ ΘΕΟΥ ἡμων ΚΑΙ ΣΩΤΗ-
ΡΟΣ ΙΗΣΟΥ ΧΡΙΣΤΟΥ.

Which, in the common English verfion, is
thus imperfectly rendered, — " *through the*
" *righteoufnefs of God and our Saviour, Jesus*
" *Chrift.*"*

This text, though *the eighth* in order, according to the proper order of the books, was
the firft example cited in my letter; and I have
only to remark farther, that the Alexandrian
MS. perfectly agrees with the prefent common
approved reading in the Greek text. In Dr
Woide's printed copy of the faid MS. there
is a point inferted after the word δικαιοσυνη,
which

---

* Note lately added by the Author. [But in the
margin (with the ufual mark of reference to the Greek
text, viz. Gr. when a more literal verfion is given) it is
properly rendered, — " *of our God and Saviour.*"]

which is not in the MS. but that is manifestly a merely-accidental typographical error.

The Reverend Mr Crutwell has remarked (in his useful edition of the English Bible with Bishop Wilson's Notes) that the words rendered in our present version, viz. *" of God " and our Saviour, Jesus' Christ,"* were rendered, *" of our God and Saviour, Jesus Christ,"* in the versions of Wickliff, Coverdale, Matthews, Cranmer, in the Bishops (Bible,) (the) Geneva, (the) Rhemish, (Bibles,) and by Doddridge, Wesley, Scattergood, and Purver; which is altogether a noble testimony of both antient and modern times against the *Socinian impiety.* The *English* reader should undoubtedly be informed of the true meaning of these words in a proper *English* idiom, as — *" Through the righteousness of Jesus Christ, our " God and Saviour: "* — which is agreeable to a literal rendering into Latin by the late learned Dr Thomas Mangey, Prebendary of Durham, viz. — *" Jesu Christi Dei et servatoris nostri."*

F 3   EXAMPLE

EXAMPLE IX.

JUDE 4.

—— καὶ ΤΟΝ μονον ΔΕΣΠΟΤΗΝ ΘΕΟΝ ΚΑΙ
ΚΥΡΙΟΝ ἡμων ΙΗΣΟΥΝ ΧΡΙΣΤΟΝ αρνȣμενοι.

This, in the common Englifh verfion, is
imperfectly rendered — " *and denying the only*
" *Lord God, and our Lord Jefus Chrift.*"

I made a tranfcript of this text, feveral years
ago, from the Alexandrian MS. which I copied,
or rather drew, letter by letter, in fize and
fhape as exactly as the eye could difcern. In
this tranfcript the word Θεον is omitted, as in
the MS. ; but I did not, at that time, perceive
that there was any point or mark after the
word Δεσποτην, and I was therefore much fur-
prifed, afterwards, in comparing the faid tranfcript with the elegant edition of my late very
worthy and refpectable friend, the Rev. Dr
Woide, (who printed a copy of the New Teftament from the Alexandrian MS. with new
types, in imitation of the letters of the MS.)
to find that he had inferted a point, in his new
edition, after the word Δεσποτην. I was very
confident that I could not difcern any fuch point,
when I examined the MS.; and yet, as I en-

tertained

tertained the higheſt reſpect and eſteem for the veracity and accuracy of Dr Woide, (of which he was, indeed, truly worthy,) it was neceſſary to have this matter properly explained; and I was rendered perfectly aware, by Dr Velthuſen's account of his examining an antient MS. that the faint lines and marks in the very old MSS. are liable to bear different appearances, according to the different degrees of light in which they are ſeen.

. I therefore took the firſt opportunity, afterwards, of going once more to examine the M S.; and, on a more cloſe inſpection, I perceived, indeed, the *faint* mark which occaſioned Dr Woide's inſertion of the period in his edition; but being afterwards aſſiſted by the worthy librarian, the Rev. Mr Harper, in a ſtill more attentive and accurate examination of the mark with a magnifying glaſs, I was ſatisfied that it had not been intended for a period, but only for a ſhort *line of connection*, becauſe it is nearly three times as long as it is broad.

But if any perſon, from the authority of Dr Woide's edition, ſhould be ſtill inclined

to

to suppose that it is really a *point*, I must request them carefully to consider what I have before remarked on the fourth, sixth, and seventh, examples in this tract, respecting the addition of *points* in Greek manuscripts; and also concerning the more accurate modes of grammatical distinction in the Greek tongue, which rendered the smaller points, or *particles of time*, (such as semicolons and commas,) absolutely unnecessary in the *Greek scripture*; and, in addition thereto, let him observe, particularly on the text before us, that a point in that place, after Δεσποτην, (in the middle of the sentence, between the accusative noun and verb,) is utterly inconsistent with grammar and common sense; and though the word Θεον has been omitted in the Alexandrian M S. (perhaps for the same reason that some men would wish to prove the insertion of the point after Δεσποτην,) yet, happily, neither of these alterations would at all affect or injure the manifest testimony of the apostle Jude *to Christ's almighty power and divinity*, for — " *the only potentate and Lord* " *of us, Jesus Christ,*" is equivalent to a full

declaration

declaration of *Chriſt's divinity*, as well as of his *almighty power*; and, with reſpect to the inſertion of the *ſuppoſed point*, they muſt perceive, if they duly conſider the text, that the words Δεσποτην and κυριον cannot (conſiſtently with the neceſſary grammatical ſenſe of the Greek, and the uſual modes of expreſſion, or idiom of that language) be ſeparated either by points or conſtruction, ſo as to be applied to two different perſons, becauſe the article is *not* repeated after the copulative, before κυριον: ſo that *Chriſt alone* was unqueſtionably that — "*only potentate*," or *ſovereign Lord*, who was denied by the *laſcivious perſons*, againſt whom the the apoſtle Jude bore teſtimony of their *reprobacy*, and of their having *denied the Lord*, who had *redeemed them*. Dr Hammond's rendering of the text before us may, therefore, be conſcientiouſly maintained, viz. "*our only Maſter, God, and Lord, Jeſus "Chriſt, *making*" (ſays he) "*thoſe three the "ſeveral attributes of Jeſus Chriſt*." — But as the Doctor has been pleaſed to add, afterwards,

* Viz. in the margin of the text; and repeated in his *Annotations*, p. 850, with the remainder of this quotation.

afterwards, — " *And this interpretation proceeds*
" *upon that way of punctuation which is ordi-*
" *narily retained in our copies, there being no*
" *comma after* Θεον, &c." I am obliged to pro-
test against *that reason, for the other reasons*
already given; and to insist, that the grammatical construction of the Greek text is, of
itself, our sufficient and best warrant to justify
that *literal rendering.*

But the applying to Christ this *supreme*
title, — " *the only potentate, God* " (and, also,
in a former text, the *supreme* title of — " *the*
" *great God"*) may, perhaps, induce some persons to conceive that this grammatical system
of construction, if admitted as a rule, for all
texts, in which the same mode of expression
renders it applicable, will sometimes prove
rather too much, and may be liable to favour a modern sect of *Unitarians,* who have
adopted the *Sabellian* notions of the late Baron
Swedenborg, and who assert, that — " *Jesus*
" *Christ is the only God;* " that is, they understand this in so peculiar a sense, that they do
not seem properly to acknowledge the *per-*
sonality of *the holy spirit,* any more than a
very

very oppofite fect of *Unitarians* do, the modern Socinians, who impioufly affert (in the oppofite extreme to that of the *Swedenborgians*) that· " *Jefus Chrift was a mere man, and nothing but a man,*" according to one of their teachers, and — " *fimple human nature,*" according to another : and fome of them have even prefumed to charge the members of the church of England with idolatry,* becaufe they pay

the

---

* This unjuft charge of *idolatry* againft the unqueftionable principles of the *antient catholic church*, profeffed by the *church of England*, affords a notable fkreen to the *Latin* church, by indifcriminately confounding all the due diftinctions whereby a charge of *idolatry* is applicable ; and this fhould teach us to be aware of what we fhould have to expect on the removal of all tefts and reftraints from fuch indifcriminate teachers ; and, likewife, from all other fectaries (as much as from the *pontifical hierarchy*, feated on the *throne of the dragon*) who do *not* regulate their faith and practice by the plain doctrines of the holy Scriptures. For, indeed, no man is juftly entitled to have a vote or fhare in the legiflature of this or any other *Chriftian* nation, unlefs he (at leaft) profeffes to regulate his *principles of action* by the *two firft foundations of* ENGLISH LAW, viz. *natural* and *revealed religion*, to which (as being *two witneffes of God*) *univerfal obedience* is due, fo that no ftatute

of

the divine honour that is due to their *Lord* and
Saviour, and to *the holy spirit,* their — " *other*
" *comforter.*

. So

of parliament can be *valid,* nor any other law, cuſtom, or
practice, *ſufferable,* if it be at all *inconſiſtent* with either of
theſe *two indiſpenſible foundations.* For, without theſe,
MEN retain, indeed, the form, but not the *dignity, of* MAN ;
becauſe they are ſubject to the impulſe of *ſpirits,* inimical
to the *nature of man ;* and are, thereby, liable to be rendered, in diſpoſition and practice, the moſt noxious of
beaſts, even — " *a generation of vipers ;* " and, therefore,
the knowledge of our own NATURE, *and of the principles of
action in* MAN, *what they are and what they ought to be,*
(which, by the Scriptures alone, is revealed to us,) is the
firſt and moſt eſſential branch of *philoſophy,* whatſoever our
modern ſceptical *philoſophers* may think to the contrary ;
for, how ſhould men be on their guard againſt any *inviſible
enemies,* of whoſe very exiſtence they are ignorant ? — But
by the holy ſcriptures we are informed, that — " *the prince*
" *of the power of the air worketh in the children of diſ-*
" *obedience ;* " — and, certainly, wherever this *Satanical
inſpiration* manifeſtly takes place among *men,* their *deſcriptive title* cannot be more accurately expreſſed than in the
terms which our Lord himſelf (as well as John the Baptiſt,
before him) applied to the haughty ſceptics whom they
oppoſed, — " *a generation of vipers,*" (Matthew xii. 34 ;)
and " *ſerpents:*" (Matthew, xxiii. 33 :) expreſſly alluding
thereby

So that both thefe fects of *Unitarians* (as well as their *Unitarian* brethren, the *Mahometans*) are, by miftaken notions of the *divine unity*, feduced from perceiving and acknowledging the declarations, throughout the holy Scriptures, of the unqueftionable exiftence of *three* divine perfons in *one* only divine nature, or *Godhead*. The old Arians

G (though

---

thereby to the *Satanical infpiration* by which they became the *children*, or *generation*, of the *old ferpent*, as our Lord plainly warned them at another time:—*Ye are of* YOUR " FATHER THE DEVIL —*and the lufts of* YOUR FA- " THER *ye will do:* — *he was a* MURDERER *from the* " *beginning, and abode not in the truth, &c."* *Men*, therefore, who will not be limited by the *two firft foundations of Englifh law*, are unworthy to be admitted to an equal participation of *civil rights* in any free *Chriftian* ftate whatever ; becaufe *true liberty* cannot be maintained without that *perfection of law* which arifes *only* from thefe *indifpenfible rules of action.*

They are *indifpenfible*, becaufe we can have no hope that our *conftitutional* eftablifhment of *natural* and *religious rights* (to " *the glory of God, peace on earth,"* and *good* " *will towards men"*) can poffibly be maintained, if fuch perfons are admitted to a fhare of *legiflative* authority, who do not acknowledge the *only foundations* on which, alone, that happy *conftitution* is built.

(though their fect was probably reprefented
by that " *fallen ftar*" which opened the
" *bottomlefs pit*" for the emiffion of the
armed locufts of the Arabian herefy, *more
ftrictly Unitarians* than themfelves*) allowed,
indeed,

* Since I wrote the above remark, refpecting the *Mahometans* and *Arians*, a more ftriking accomplifhment of
the prophecy, refpecting the *fallen ftar that opened the
bottomlefs pit*, has occured to me, in the character of *Neftorius*, Archbifhop of Conftantinople and metropolitan of
the Greek church, whofe doctrine was, in effect, ftill
" *more Unitarian than*" that of *Arius* ; for, the confequences of his denying the miraculous birth of our Lord,
and afferting that — " *Chrift born of the Virgin Mary was
not the fon of God ;*" muft neceffarily be, that he was —
" *a mere man,*" and — " *nothing but a man,*" according
to the openly-declared notions of our modern Socinians,
which, in this point, is ftrictly *Mahometan!* With this
falfe and *antichriftian* doctrine " *the third part of the
rivers and fountains of waters*" (viz. the fources of
the nations and the *people* of the *Greek* Empire, the *third*
great monarchy) was *embittered* and prepared for the *fcor-
pion*-like fcourge of *Mahometan* tyranny.

On account of this blafphemous doctrine, *Neftorius* was
depofed (by the judgement of a great counfel of his *peers,
the Chriftian bifhops)* from his dignity as *Archbifhop* of the
greateft city (at that time) in Chriftendom, and from
being

indeed, that *Chriſt was God*, yet they ſuppoſed him to be ſo, in *an inferior degree*; by which

they

being *metropolitan*, as it were, of the *Greek Empire*, (the *third* great monarchy ;) and, therefore, he might truly be ſaid to have *fallen* from the higheſt elevation of eccleſiaſtical dignity ; ſo that no prophetical type could more amply prefigure this rejection than — " *the fallen ſtar* " *from heaven*," — the heaven or *firmament* of the then-amply *eſtabliſhed* epiſcopal authority throughout the Roman empire. And the *Unitarian* doctrine of this *fallen ſtar* (I mean *Unitarian* in the *Mahometan* and *Socinian* ſenſe of that term) ſeems alſo to have been the *very* " *key*," whereby " *the bottomleſs pit* " was opened to let out the noxious and diabolical vapour of *Mahometaniſm ;* for, it is really *the leading* and firſt inculcated tenet in all the public profeſſions of that baneful hereſy. And it is re-markable that a *Neſtorian* monk, *Sergius*, profeſſing the ſame blaſphemous doctrine, (this — " *key of the bottomleſs* " *pit* " forged by *Neſtorius,)* ſhould actually have been an aſſiſtant to *Mahomet*, in producing his pretended reve-lations ; and it is ſtill more remarkable, that all the *ſcor-pion-like* ſcourges of *Mahometan* conqueſt (firſt, LAWLESS TYRANNY and the ſuppreſſion of all *popular rights ;* ſe-condly, ROBBERY and WAR notoriouſly ſanctioned or authorized by this pretended religion againſt *all* nations and people that do not receive their doctrine ; and, thirdly, the fatal *renewal* of the old *pagan* oppreſſions of *ſlave-holding*

they unwarily acknowledged a *superior God*,
and an *inferior God:* i. e. *more Gods* than *one*,
contrary

holding and *slave-dealing*,* which had been happily extin-
guished by the general influence of *Christian* benevolence)
should have completely pervaded all those eastern and
southern regions of the *third* Empire, wherever the doctrines of *Nestorius* had been previously adopted, and had
embittered the *rivers* and *fountains* of the waters, to pre-
pare them for this signal *retribution*, justly due to such
antichristian apostates, who deny the true *rock* on which
the *Catholic church* is built, viz. that " *Jesus is the Christ,*
" *the son of the living God;* " or, as St John has expressed
the *peculiar sonship*, or filiation, of Christ, viz. " *the* ONLY
" BEGOTTEN SON, *which is in the bosom of the Father.*"
John, i. 18, compare with ver. 14, and chap. iii. 16
and 18.

All the arguments produced by the learned *Vitringa*, to
prove that *Arius* was the *fallen star*, are certainly much
more applicable to *Nestorius*, as being an *archbishop* and
metropolitan

---

* Such diabolical enormities may surely be compared to the dark
exhalations of — " *the bottomless pit;* " and, therefore, our English
promoters of *slave-holding* and *slave-dealing* (who have carried these
Mahometan oppressions to a greater excess even than the *Mahometans*
themselves) have ample reason to dread the approaching time of *divine
retribution*, when God will — " *destroy the destroyers of the earth,*"
and shall cause those that now — " *lead into captivity* " (and, surely,
likewise, all their abettors) — " *to be led into captivity!* "

contrary to the *true Unitarian doctrine* of *the primitive churches,* which always held and asserted *the unity of God* (like the church of England to this day) as much as they held it necessary to acknowledge the *three divine persons:* both of which doctrines are inevitable and indispensable while we profess to regulate our faith by the testimonies of the holy Scriptures, as handed down to us, without presuming to exercise the Socinian expedient of lopping off, or altering, (as a supposed *corruption* or *interpolation,)* every text of Scripture that opposes the system or set of notions that we happen to have adopted. And, therefore, the *true Unitarian* Christian, who acknowledges but *one God, one Jehovah, one divine nature,* (Θεοτης,) or *Godhead,* and at the same time, nevertheless, is convinced, that *three divine persons* are really re-

G 3   vealed

---

metropolitan of the empire, and therefore more fitly prefigured by a *star.* And that the smoke from — " *the bottomless pit,*" which was let out by this *fallen star,* was really the mist or diabolical darkness of *Mahometanism,* seems to have been fairly proved by our learned countryman, Joseph Mede.

vealed to us under the title of *Jehovah** in the old teftament, and under the title of Θεος, or *God,* in the New Teftament; and that the *fupreme attributes* of the DIVINE NATURE are applied to each, in both Teftaments; will, of courfe, be aware, alfo, that each of thefe divine perfons muft neceffarily be " *the* " *great God"* and " *the only potentate,"* as there is but " *one God,"* *one only fupreme power* or *Godhead.*

So that the effect of my grammatical rule,† when applied to the two particular texts before-mentioned, (viz. Tit. ii. 13, and Jude, 4,) will not (in the opinion of fuch true Chriftians) feem to exceed the truth.

Though the apoftle Paul afferted to the Coloffians, (ii. 9,) concerning Chrift, that " *in him dwelleth* ALL *the fulnefs of the God-* " *head,"*

---

* I need not, here, recite the proofs of thefe affertions becaufe I have already produced a great variety of examples, collected from the Old as well as the New Teftament, in my tract on the " *Law of nature and principles* " *of action in man,"* from p. 234 to p. 301.

† Compared with the concurrent reafons and teftimonies quoted in the note, p. 24. EDITOR.

" *head*," (της Θεοτητος,) " *bodily*," (σωματικως,
a term of indifputable *perfonality*,) yet, furely,
this was without the leaft difparagement to
the fupreme divinity of the *Almighty Father*,
and of the *Holy Spirit*, becaufe they are, alfo,
neceffarily included in the fame Θεοτης, or
Godhead, as there is but *cne God*; and, therefore, as " *it pleafed all fulnefs to dwell*" in the
perfon of our *Lord Jefus Chrift*, (Col. i. 19,)
we may more eafily comprehend why he required, " *that all*" (men) " *fhould honour*
" *the fon*, EVEN AS *they honour the Father*;"
that is, undoubtedly, *with fupreme honour*,
καθως, EVEN AS, or *according as*, " *they ho-*
" *nour the father*. And our Lord faid, expreffly, " *he that honoureth not the fon* (that
is, according to the meafure before declared, " EVEN AS *they honour*," or *ought to
honour, the father*) " *honoureth not the father*
" *which hath fent him*; (John, v. 23;) and
he alfo claimed expreffly *to be glorified with
the father himfelf*. " *And now, O father*, (faid
he,) " GLORIFY THOU ME WITH THINE OWN-
" SELF, *with the glory which I had with thee
" before the world was*;" (John, xvii. 5;)
thereby

thereby afferting both his *pre-exiftence* and *fupreme dignity.* Chriftians, therefore, who humbly receive thefe and the many other revelations of *Chrift's divinity,* have the lefs difficulty in acknowledging the *doctrines of the antient catholic churches* and the declarations of our *creeds.* But let all other men, likewife, who profefs to believe in the *name of Chrift,* earneftly inquire, in the *firft* place, as the *firft* means of progrefs to the true faith, whether they are really " *willing* " (for this is given as the true proof of *faith,* εαν τις θελη,) to conform themfelves to the *will of God,* as revealed in all the moft obvious declarations and injunctions of holy Scripture, and more particularly to the purity, which is exprefsly called " *the will of* " *God,*" viz. the *fanctification of their bodies,**

which

* " For this is the *will of God,* even your fanctification, " that you fhould abftain from fornication: that every one " of you fhould know how to poffefs his veffel in *fanctifica-* " *tion* and *honour;* not in the luft of concupifcence, even " as the Gentiles, which know not God: that no one " fhould go beyond or defraud his brother, &c." I. Theff. iv. 3, 6.

which cannot otherwife be capable of becoming " *temples of the Holy Ghoft :*" an
indifpenfable ftate both of *body* and *mind* for
all Chriftians to maintain; for, in that cafe,
they may affuredly rely on God's abfolute
promife, through Chrift, that " *if any one*
" *fhall be* WILLING *to do* HIS WILL, *he fhall*
" *know of the doctrine, whether it be of God, or*
" *whether I fpeak*" (faid our Lord) " *from*
" *myfelf.*" (John, vii. 17.)

DEO SOLI GLORIA.

INDEX

To the Texts cited in the preceding Work.

Abbreviations: r. *rule.* — g. e. *general exception.* — p. e. *particular exception.* — n. *note.*

i.   4, r. 1 . . 6
—   — . . 29 n.

Ephesians.

i.   2, r. 5 . . 13
—   3, r. 1 . . 29 n.
ii.   2 . . . 60 n.
iv.   6, g.e. to r. 5, 14
—   — r. 1 . . 29 n.
—   — g.e. to r. 5, 14
—   31, r. 5 . . 13
v.   5, r. 1 . . 30
—   20, — . . 6
—   — . . 29 n.
—   20, 21, r. 3 . 10
vi.   21, r. 1 . . 4
—   23, r. 5 . . 13

Philemon.

—   3, r. 5 . . 13

Philipians.

iii.   3, r. 1 . . 32
iv.   20, r. 1 . . 4
—   — . . 29 n.

Colossians.

i.   3 and 12, r. 1   6
—   3, r. 1 . . 29 n.
—   16 . . . 11 n.
—   17 . . . 11 n.
—   19 . . . 67
—   27 . . . 25 n.
ii.   2, r. 1, . 4, 29 n.
—   — r. 6, 15 . 15
—   — g.e. to r. 2, 10
—   9 . . . 7
—   9 . . . 66
iii.   17, r. 1 . . 6
—   — . . 29 n.

I. Thess.

i.   3, r. 1 . . 6
—   — . . 29 n.
iii.   6, g.e. to r. 6, 15

iii.   11, r. 1 . . 4, 14 n.
—   — — . . 29 n.
—   13, — . . 6
—   — — . . 29
iv.   3, 6 . . . 68

II. Thess.

i.   12, r. 1 . . 34
—   — . . 50
ii.   8 . . . 25 n.
—   16, r. 1 . . 6
—   — — . . 29

I. Tim.

i.   1 . . . 25 n.
—   — r. 3 . . 11
—   2, r. 4 . . 11
v.   21, r. 1 . . 38
—   — — . . 42
—   — — . . 45 n.
—   — — . . 49 n.
vi.   14 . . . 25 n.

II. Tim.

i.   2, r. 4 . . 11
—   5, r. 6 . . 15
—   10 . . . 25 n.
iv.   1, r. 1 . 41, 50
—   — — . . 49 n.
—   1 and 8 . . 25 n.

Titus.

i.   1, r. 3 . . 11
—   — . . 15 n.
—   4, r. 4 . . 11
ii.   13, r. 1 . . 22
—   — — . . 50
—   — — . . 66
—   — — . . 24 n.

Heb.

i.   2 . . . 11 n.
iii.   1, r. 1 . . 4
xiii.   20, r. 2 . . 8, 9

James.

	James.	
i.	1	12 n.
—	— p.e. to r. 5,	13 n.
—	————,	17
i.	27, r. 1 . .	5
—	——— . . .	29 n.
iii.	9, r. 1 . .	6
—	——— . . .	29
	I. Pet.	
i.	3, r. 1 . .	29 n.
ii.	17	11 n.
iv.	11, r. 6 . .	15
v.	4	8 n.
	II. Pet.	
i.	1, r. 1 . .	20,52
ii.	20, — . .	4
iii.	2, — . .	4
—	18, — . .	4

	II. John.	
iii.	3, r. 4 . .	11
	Jude.	
	4, r. 1 . .	54,66
	Rev.	
i.	6, r. 1 . .	6
—	8, g.e. to r. 5,	18
—	——— r. 6,	18
—	17, g.e. to r. 6,	17
ii.	8, ————,	18
viii.	10 to 12 . .	64 n.
ix.	1 to 12 . .	62 n.
—	2, . . .	63 n.
—	2, (2d note)	64
xvi.	15, r. 1 . .	4
xx.	2, g.e. to r. 5,	19
xxii.	13, ———	18
—	—, g.e. to r. 6,	19

INDEX

Chrift

D.

Neftorius,

N.

O.

P.

R.

ERRATUM.

P. 25, l. 6, μεγελου for μεγαλου.

APPENDIX.

I.

A TABLE of EVIDENCES

OF

CHRIST's DIVINITY,

FROM

Dr WHITBY's

COMM. on the NEW TESTAMENT.

II.

A PLAIN ARGUMENT,

FROM THE

GOSPEL-HISTORY,

FOR THE

DIVINITY of CHRIST,

BY

THE EDITOR OF THE TWO FIRST EDITIONS.

*Extract from Dr Whitby's third Discourse, sub-
joined to his Last Thoughts.*

"THAT our Lord Jesus Christ is true God, as having
"true dominion over all things in heaven and earth
"delivered to him from the Father, and as having all
"divine excellencies which are necessary to enable him
"to exercise dominion while this world lasts, and at the
"close of the world to make manifest the secrets of all
"hearts, and to render to every man according as his
"works shall be, has been fully proved in my Last
"Thoughts, Sect. 4 and 5."

Discourse III. p. 143, subjoined to his *Last Thoughts.*

A TABLE

OF

EVIDENCES

OF

CHRIST's DIVINITY.*

THE divine nature of Chrift may be proved,

I. From John, i. 1, 2, 3. v. 21, 22, 23.
viii. 58. x. 30. xii. 41. xvi. 14, 15.
xviii. 5. xx. 28. Luke, i. 43.

II. From his titles, he being
1. Jehovah, Rom. x. 13.
2. God, Rom. xiv. 12. I. Cor. x. 9. Heb. i. 8. and iii. 4.
3. The true God, I. John, v. 20.
4. God manifefted in the flefh, I. Tim. iii. 16.
5. The great God, Tit. ii. 13.
6. God over all, bleffed for ever, Rom. ix. 5.
7. The Lord of all, Rom. x. 12.

The

* For the details of thefe evidences fee Dr Whitby's Commentary on the feveral paffages here quoted.

The divine nature of Chrift may be proved,

III. From the divine worfhip afcribed to him, he being the object of religious adoration and invocation, Rom. x. 13. Col. iii. 24. II. Theff. iii. 16. Acts, vii. 59. Acts, ix. 14. Compare Matt. iv. 10, with John, v. 23, and Heb. i. 6.

IV. From the divine actions and attributes afcribed to him, he being

1. Omnifcient, John, ii. 25, xxi. 17. The fearcher of all hearts, I. Cor. iv. 5.

2. Omnipotent, Philip. iii. 21.

3. The raifer of all men from the dead, Col. i. 19.

4. Who raifed himfelf from the dead, John, ii. 19. x. 18.

5. The Creator of all things, John, i. 3. Col. i. 16. Heb. i. 2, 10,

6. The upholder of all things, Col. i. 17. Heb. i. 3.

7. Who was in the form of God, and was God before he was made man, Philip. ii. 6. John, i. 1.

8. In whom dwelt all the fulnefs of the Godhead bodily, Col. i. 19. ii. 9.

A

A PLAIN ARGUMENT,*

FROM THE

GOSPEL-HISTORY,

FOR THE

DIVINITY of CHRIST.

QUESTION.

FOR what END *did Chriſt* COME INTO THE WORLD?

A. " Chriſt came into the world to ſave " ſinners." (I. Tim. i. 15.)

Q. How do you mean " to ſave ſinners?"

A. To ſave them from the power of ſin here, and the everlaſting puniſhment of it hereafter.

Q. How muſt we be ſaved from the everlaſting puniſhment of ſin?

A. By Chriſt's DEATH. He was " mani-" feſted in the fleſh," that is, was made man,

I   to

---

* Reprinted from the ſecond Edition of *a Chriſtmas Gift*.

to DIE, and to be "THE PROPITIATION, for
" the fins of the whole world." "By his own
" blood Chrift obtained eternal redemption for
" us." (I. Cor. xv. 3. I. John, ii. 2. Heb.
ix. 12.)

Q. *How muft we be delivered from the pow-*
er of fin here?

A. By " the fpirit of Chrift." (Rom.
viii. 9.) " For he came to deftroy the works
" of the devil, to redeem us from all iniquity,
" and to purify unto himfelf a peculiar people
" zealous of good works." (I. John, iii. 8.
Tit. ii. 14.)

Q. *Muft we not alfo ufe our own moft earneft*
endeavours ?

A. Yes. We muft " watch and pray" a-
gainft all temptation to fin; (Matt. xxvi. 41.
Mark, xiii. 13;) and ftudy God's word that
we may be fanctified by it. (John, xvii. 17.)

Q. *Could no one fave finners but Chrift ?*

A. No. " There is none other name un-
" der heaven given among men, whereby we
" muft be faved." (Acts, iv. 12.)

Q. *Could not Chrift fave finners without*
dying for their fins?

A.

A. No.

Q. Why could not man's redemption be accomplished without the death of Christ?

A. Because it was the will of God, and fore-ordained by God, that Christ should die for the sins of the world.

Q. How do you know that Christ's death was fore-ordained by God?

A. Because it was fore-told by the prophets.

Q. Have you any other reason for believing that Christ's death was necessary for our salvation?

A. I believe that without Christ's death there could have been no salvation, because we are assured, by the holy spirit, in the words of St Paul, that " without shedding of " blood there is no remission" of sins. (Heb. ix. 22.)

Q. Have you any other reason?

A. Yes. The INCARNATION of Christ, that is, Christ's *being made man*, and *being born into the world*, seems also to be a proof that his death was necessary for our salvation. For he who " in the beginning was

I 2   " with

" with God, and was God," was " made
" flefh," and " took upon him the form,"
that is, the nature " and likenefs, of man,"
on purpofe, as it feems, that he might " be-
" come obedient unto death," (and thus might
be capable of dying,) " even the death of the
crofs." (John, i. 1. Philipp. ii. 6, 7, 8.)

§. 2.

Q. *Where was Chrift before he came into
this world, and was manifefted in the flefh?*

A. He was in Heaven. " He came down
" from Heaven. He was with God, his Father,
" before the world was, before the founda-
" tion of the world: he was in the bofom of
" his Father, and in his Father's glory." —
(John, iii. 13. — vi. 33, 62. — i. 1. — xvii.
5, 24. — i. 18. — xvii. 5.)

§. 3.

Q. *How was Chrift's manifeftation in the
flefh made known to the world?*

A. By the meffage of an angel, who declared to Mary, his mother, and to Jofeph,
what manner of child it fhould be that
fhould

ſhould be born of her, and at his birth proclaimed him to certain ſhepherds.

Q. *Where was Chriſt born?*

A. In Bethlehem of Judea. (Matt. ii. 1,
5, 6.)

Q. *Under what name was he made known?*

A. He was called JESUS, a Saviour, the
Son of God, the Son of the Higheſt.

Q. *Who was the mother of Jeſus?*

A. The Virgin Mary.

Q. *Was any prophecy fulfilled by the birth
of Jeſus Chriſt?*

A. Yes. " All this was done that it might
" be fulfilled, which was ſpoken of the Lord
" by the prophet, ſaying, behold a virgin
" ſhall be with child, and ſhall bring forth a
" ſon, and they ſhall call his name EMMANU-
" EL, which, being interpreted, is GOD WITH
us." (Matt. i. 22, 23. Iſaiah, vii. 14.)

§. 4.

Q. *What was Chriſt put to death for?*

A. For blaſphemy, as the Jews thought it,
in calling himſelf the Son of God.

I 3   Q.

Q. *In what did the Jews say the blasphemy consisted?*

A. In this, that he, being, as they supposed, a mere man, called God his own Father, thereby declaring himself to be equal with God, and to be very God. (John, v. 18. x. 33.)

§. 5.

Q. *What did Christ ever say of himself, which implied that he was God?*

A. He said that he was one with God, and partook of the glory of God, before the world was, that is, from all eternity.

Catechift. *Repeat the passage in which he said that he partook of the glory of God before the world was.*

A. " And now, O Father, glorify thou me " with thine ownself, with the glory which I " had with thee before the world was." (John xvii. 5.)

Q. *What did Christ ever say of himself, which implied that he was equal with God?*

A. He said that " he and his Father are " one:" that " the Father had given all things " into

" into his hand:" that " what things foever
" the Father doeth, thefe alfo doeth the Son
" likewife :" that " the Father hath com-
" mitted all judgement to the Son, that all
" men fhould honour the Son, even as they
" honour the Father:" (John x. 30.—iii. 35.
—v. 19.—v. 22.)

§ 6.

Q. *Where do we find the firft evidences of
Chrift's Divinity ?*

A. In the antient prophets, Ifaiah, (vii.
14.) Jeremiah, (xxiii. 6.) and Daniel, (vii.
14.) where he is called " Immanuel," that
is, GOD with us : " The Lord," that is,
" JEHOVAH, " our righteoufnefs:" and his
" dominion" is declared to be an " EVER-
" LASTING dominion."

Q. *Who, in Chrift's time, firft bore teftimony
to his divinity ?*

A. The angel, who at his birth proclaimed
him to the fhepherds, as " Chrift, THE
" LORD :" The fhepherds who made known
this faying that was told them: And the
Demoniacks,

Demoniacks, who acknowledged him to be
THE SON OF GOD. (Mark, iii. 11.)

Q. *Who were the first witnesses to Christ's
own testimony of his divinity?*

A. His enemies, the unbelieving Jews,
both the people, and their rulers.

Q. *How were the unbelieving Jews witnesses
to Christ's testimony of himself?*

A. By reporting and interpreting his words.

Q. *Do you call the unbelieving Jews earlier
witnesses than the Apostles?*

A. Yes: because the apostles appear not
to have known that Christ was God, till after his Resurrection and Ascension into heaven.

Q. *In what manner was the Divinity of
Christ unfolded to the world in Christ's time?*

A. An angel proclaimed it at his birth;
the shepherds reported it; the Demoniacks
confessed it. Christ afterwards asserted himself to be God, by calling God his own
Father, and himself the Son of God, in a
sense, which implied, that he was equal
with God, and was God;—so even his unbelieving hearers understood him:—the Jews
condemned

condemned him to death for it : — the Apoſtles, after his Reſurrection and Aſcenſion, preached it to the world.

§ 7.

Q. As Chriſt knew that this was the ſenſe in which the Jews underſtood his teſtimony of himſelf, when they firſt charged him with blaſphemy for it,—did he, at his trial, attempt to deny the charge?

A. No: he admitted the charge, and confirmed it, and died for it; and appealed to the day of judgement as their future proof of it.

Q. What are Chriſt's words?

A. When " the high Prieſt aſked him, " and ſaid unto him, art thou the Son of the " Bleſſed? Jeſus ſaid, I am ; and *(as a proof* " *that I am)* ye ſhall *(at the day of judgement)* " ſee *(me)* the Son of Man, ſitting at the " right hand of power, *(that is, at the right* " *hand of God.)* and coming in the clouds of " heaven." (Mark xiv. 61, 62.)

Q. If Chriſt had not been the Meſſiah, the Son of God, in the ſenſe in which they un-
derſtood

derſtood him, would he not have undeceived them?

A. If Chriſt had not been the Meſſiah, the Son of God, in the ſenſe in which the Jews underſtood him, he would have undeceived them, to ſave his own life, and to free them from a very great deluſion.

Q. *But Chriſt was put to Death for calling himſelf the Son of God; what then do you conclude?*

A. I conclude that Jeſus Chriſt really was what they charged him with calling himſelf, THE SON OF GOD; and in the ſenſe in which they underſtood him; that is, that he was EQUAL WITH GOD, and therefore was VERY GOD.

§. 8.

Q. *You ſay that in the lifetime of Chriſt the Apoſtles appeared not to know that Chriſt was God: where do you find this?*

A. It appears from their expecting a temporal deliverer inſtead of a ſpiritual one; and from their not knowing, till after the Reſurrection

rection and ascension of Christ, the end of his coming into the world.

Q. *Where do you learn that, before the re-surrection and ascension of Christ, his disciples did not know the end of his coming into the world?*

A. I learn it from Christ's rebuke of St Peter. (Matt. xvi. 23.)

Q. *Where do you learn that they expected a temporal deliverer?*

A. I learn it from the acknowledgement of the two disciples, (who were going to Emmaus,) that their hopes of his being their deliverer were disappointed by his death; (Luke xxiv. 21.) and from their inquiring of Christ, soon after his resurrection, if he would, at that time, restore the kingdom to Israel. (Acts i. 6.)

Q. *What was their opinion of Christ after his resurrection and ascension into heaven?*

A. Convinced partly by his resurrection from the dead, according to his promise that he would *raise himself* from the dead, and, fully instructed by the Holy Spirit after his ascension, they believed him to be " their
" Lord

" Lord and their God," — " the Word made
" flefh;" " God manifeft in the flefh ;" in
whom " dwelt ALL the fulnefs of the God-
" head bodily;" " Emmanuel," or, " God
" with us," — " the creator and upholder of
" all things," who " in the beginning" of all
things, " was with God, and was God;" —
" the true God and eternal life ;" and " over
" all God bleffed for ever." (John xx. 28.
i. 14. 1 Tim. iii. 16. Col. ii. 9. Matt.
i. 23. John i. 3. Col. i. 17. Heb. i. 3.
John i. 1. — 1. John v. 20. Rom. ix. 5.*)

§. 9.

Q. *Now, tell me, in few words, what you
conclude from Chrift's teftimony of himfelf, as
attefted by the Jews of his own time, condemned
by their rulers, but univerfally declared by the
apoftles.*

A.

---

* Whatever difficulty may be found in the various
readings of any of thefe paffages, it muft vanifh in the
full light of their united evidence. To them we may
confidently add the very important teftimonies, which,
in the preceeding remarks and examples, Mr Sharp has
moft happily recovered from the erroneous conftructions
of the common Englifh verfion.

A. I conclude that Chriſt, the Son of God, is one with God, and equal with God, both in nature, and power, and in glory, and therefore is very God. Chriſt aſſerted it; the Jews condemned him to die for it; he ſealed his teſtimony with his blood. The apoſtles, partly convinced by his reſurrection from the dead, and fully inſtructed by the Holy Spirit after his aſcenſion into heaven, believed it, and preached it, and died for it.

§. 10.

Catechiſt. *The Jews, then, put Chriſt to death as an impoſtor and blaſphemer; and yet Chriſtians have believed in him, and worſhipped him, as the Son of God, for almoſt eighteen hundred years. How do you account for this?*

A. It was the will of God that Chriſt ſhould die for the ſins of mankind. If the Jews had believed him to be the Son of God they would not have put him to death; — if he had not been put to death as he was he would not have " borne our ſins

K   " in

"in his own body on the crofs;" that is, he would not have died for our fins, THE END FOR WHICH HE CAME INTO THE WORLD: —he would not have given that great and ineftimable proof of the truth of Scripture, and of his own promifes, which HE did, by rifing from the dead: — and the Apoftles would not have given that fure evidence of their own belief in Chrift, (the ground and confirmation of OURS,) which THEY did, by dying for their crucified Lord and Mafter.

APPENDIX

APPENDIX the THIRD.

CONTAINING

EXTRACTS

FROM

THE UNDERMENTIONED REVIEWS.

The British Critic for January, 1800.
———————————— for July, 1802.
The Christian Observer for July, 1802.
The Christian Guardian for December, 1802.
The Orthodox Churchman for February, 1803.

EXTRACTS, &c.

EXTRACT from the BRITISH CRITIC for January, 1800. No. I. of vol. xv p. 70, art. xii.

" The defign of the —— —— author, Mr G. Sharp, is to demonftrate the divinity of our Saviour by fhowing, that, in feveral paffages of the New Teftament, tranflated as they ought to be, according to ftrict grammatical analogy, that article of our faith is expreffly and pofitively afferted; though that affertion has, in our common verfion, difappeared for want of a correct rendering of the original. The fix rules laid down for this purpofe, the accuracy of which is proved in various ways, and particularly by the conduct of our tranflators on other occafions, we extracted at large in our notice of the Mufeum Oxonienfe; but we fhall now recur to them, becaufe, in the table of contents here prefixed, we obferve fuch an abftract of them, and of the examples, as to a fcholar almoft fufficiently explains the whole argument, its force, and application. The firft rule is moft important, being more extenfive in its application than the reft; to this, therefore, we particularly call the reader's attention. It is thus ftated in the table of contents, more briefly, but perhaps more clearly, than in the body of the work," &c.

After citing feveral examples of the firft rule, the Britifh Critic adds as follows, in p. 72. — " The examples here cited are by no means all that have the fame tendency, but they are the moft remarkable; and the remaining rules appear no lefs folid than the firft. It fhould be obferved, alfo, that, in feveral inftances more than we have mentioned, the verfion recommended by Mr G. S. has the fanction of feveral early tranflators and commentators.

And

And he concludes, in p. 73, with the following obfervations on the appendix, viz. "The part fubjoined to
Mr G. Sharp's remarks by the learned Editor, entitled
' a plain matter-of-fact argument,' &c. turns on this circumftance, that our Saviour was actually condemned to
death by the Jews for blafphemy, in afferting his own
Godhead; and that, inftead of denying the circumftance,
he confirmed it, and fealed his teftimony with his blood.
It is thrown into the form of queftion and anfwer, in order to be ufed in catechetical inftruction, and is drawn up
with great precifion, clearnefs, and cogency of reafon."

Remarks of the BRITISH CRITIC for July, 1802,
No. I. of vol. xx. p. 15, art. iv.
*Six Letters to Granville Sharp, Efq. refpecting his Remarks
on the ufes of the Definite Article in the Greek Text of the
New Teftament.*
" A great acceffion of authority, and, we truft, a pro-
portionable increafe of celebrity, will be given, by thefe
acute and learned letters, to the Remarks of Mr Granville Sharp on the Greek article, which, in our 15th vol.
(p. 70,) we introduced to public notice, as of the higheft
utility and importance.* Thofe remarks, it muft be
recollected, are not merely of a philological nature, as the
title might feem to imply; but, by means of a clear
idiom and analogy of the Greek language, eftablifh certain texts of the New Teftament, as invincible barriers
againft the doctrines and fubterfuges of Socinian teachers.
" This account applies principally to the firft rule laid
down in the Remarks, to which alfo the letters now an-
nounced refer; and we muft remind or inform our readers,
                                                    that

---

* " A fecond edition of Mr Granville Sharp's Remarks
has very recently been publifhed by the original editor,
Mr Burgefs, Prebendary of Durham, and is fold by
Vernor and Hood, Rivingtons, and Hatchard. As, ac-
cidentally, we have not the former edition at hand, to
make an accurate comparifon between them, we fhall not
at prefent give a feparate article on the new edition, nor
at all, unlefs we find the alterations important."

that by the natural and neceſſary operation of this rule are produced theſe texts : ' according to the grace of Jeſus Chriſt, *our God* and Lord ;' (2 Theſſ. i. 12;) ' waiting for the glorious appearance of *our great God and Saviour,* Jeſus Chriſt;' (Titus, ii. 13;) and ſome others of ſimilar force ; in which paſſages, by the vicious neglect of the rule, God and Chriſt have been ſeparated into two perſons, in our public verſion, contrary to the intention of the original writer, and the undoubted idiom of the language in which he wrote.*

" According to our own opinion, formed with the ſtricteſt attention to the evidence produced, this rule, as ſtated by Mr Sharp, appeared perfectly clear, and the deductions from it no leſs than inevitable. We conſidered it as founded in truth and demonſtrated with ability. But we ſee, with much additional ſatisfaction, the explicit teſtimony of ſo great a maſter of Greek literatute as Mr Burgeſs, ſtated in the ſecond edition of the Remarks. His opinion was before implied in the act of publiſhing the Remarks, and was otherwiſe intimated in the firſt edition; but it is now, in an introductory letter to Mr Sharp, expreſſed in the ſtrongeſt terms.

' That you have happily and deciſively applied your rule of conſtruction to the correction of the common Engliſh verſion of the New Teſtament, and to the *perfect eſtabliſhment* of the great doctrine in queſtion, the DIVINITY of CHRIST, no impartial reader, I think, can doubt, *who is at all acquainted with the original language of the New Teſtament.'*

" When it is conſidered that the writer who gives this teſtimony is Mr Burgeſs, whoſe knowledge of the Greek language qualified him, very early in life, to produce a
much

---

* " The rule may be thus briefly and looſely expreſſed, though to be ſtrictly accurate it will require, as Mr Sharp has given it, more limitations. " When two nouns deſcriptive of a perſon, and united by a conjunction, have only one article prefixed to both, they are both intended to deſcribe the ſame perſon.' This rule is uniformly followed by all Greek writers.''

much improved edition of one of the acutest books we have on Greek literature, *Dawes's Miscellanea Critica;* and who, from that time to this, has distinguished himself by various works illustrative of the Greek language and the authors who have used it, the force and value of the decision may be duly estimated. Speaking farther of the rule in question, the same learned editor says to Mr Sharp, ' I call the rule *yours;* for, though it was acknowledged and applied by Beza and others * to some of the texts alleged by you, yet never was it so prominently, because singly, or so effectually, as in your Remarks.' This testimony of Theodore Beza, an acknowledged scholar, and a translator of the whole New Testament, is particularly valuable; and, as it has not been given at length, in what has hitherto been published, we shall here insert it. In commenting on the text, Tit. ii. 13, επιφανειαν της δοξης τυ μιγαλυ Θευ και Σωτηρος ημων Ιησυ

---

* " Beza is not the only one among the biblical critics who has noticed this idiom; it has occasionally been urged by various writers. Abundant praise is due to Mr Granville Sharp for bringing it forward in the distinct manner he has, and for illustrating it by so great a variety of apposite examples; but we must not, if we would be correct, consider it as his discovery even among the moderns. Wolfius says, ' Articulus τυ praemittendus fuisset voci Σωτηρος (in Tit. ii. 13) siquidem hic a μιγαλυ Θευ distingui debuisset.' *In loco.* Drusius, on the same text, says, " Non solum Deus, sed etiam *Deus Magnus,* vocatur hic Christus' (in Crit. Sacro); where, though the rule is not mentioned, it is taken for granted as undeniable Bishop Bull, Calovius, Vitringa, and Dr Twells, are all referred to by Wolfius, as supporting this sense, on the verse of Titus above-mentioned : and Erasmus, who speaks of that passage as ambiguous, had too much knowledge of Greek not to own, that the omission of the article had some force against that opinion. ' Quanquam *omissus articulus,* in libris Græcis, facit *nonnihil* pro diversa sententiâ. Μιγαλυ Θευ και Σωτηρος, evidentius distinxisset personas si dixisset, και τυ Σωτηρος,' *Rev.*"

Ιησυ Χριςυ, after fpeaking of the επιφανεια, which he rightly infifts muft belong to Chrift, and which he tranflates
adventus, he thus proceeds: ' Quod autem ad alterum
attinet quum fcriptum fit, ε. τυ μεγαλυ Θευ και Σωτηρος ημων
I. X. non autem τυ μεγαλυ Θευ και τυ Σωτηρος, dico non
magis probabiliter ifta poffe ad duas diftinctas perfonas referri, quam illam locutionem ὁ Θεος και Πατηρ Ιησυ Χριςυ.
Nam id certe poftulat Græci fermonis ufus, *quum unus
tantum fit articulus*, *duobus iftis*, nempe Θευ και Σωτηρος,
Θεος και Πατηρ, *communis*: quum præfertim, ut antè dixi,
nunquam επιφανεια aut παρυσια nifi uni Filio tribuatur.
Itaque fic concludo, Chriftum Jefum hic apertè Magnum
Deum dici, qui et beata illa fpes noftra metonymicè vocatur. Illi igitur ut verè magno et æterno Deo, fit
gloria et laus omnis, in fæcula fæculorum.' Here the
rule, refpecting the article, is diftinctly laid down, as by
Mr Sharp, and the fame conclufion, with equal diftinct-
nefs, drawn.

"But the authority of Beza, or of any modern, was
not fufficient for the ingenious writer of thefe Six Letters.[*]
He thought of a higher appeal, to the Greek Fathers;
as men who could not but be competent judges of their
native language. ' If Mr Sharp's rule be true,' faid he,
' then will *their* interpretation of thofe texts be invariably
in the fame fenfe in which he underftands them,' p. 3.
To thefe judges, then, he appealed; and, by a moft laborious examination of their works, has produced fuch an
additional teftimony, in behalf of the rule, as cannot fail
to aftonifh thofe who are moft unwilling to be convinced.
When we think of examining, for a few texts, the voluminous works of feventy Greek and near fixty Latin
Fathers and other divines, befides theological collections
of great magnitude, we think of a labour which refem-
bles rather the indefatigable diligence of former times
than the fupinenefs of modern refearch. Yet fuch was the
                                                        origin

---

[*] "This writer we learn, on inquiry, to be Mr C.
Wordfworth, of Trinity-college, Cambridge; who,
though he modeftly withheld his name at firft, is not, we
underftand, anxious to be concealed."

origin of the prefent volume," (the 6 letters,) "and fuch
the induftry and acutenefs employed to furnifh the materials.

"In the fequel to Mr Sharp's remarks are nine examples of his firft rule, eight of which are fuch as muft, by
their genuine application, introduce important alterations
in the verfion, and become, only by being rightly tranflated, direct affertions of the Divinity of Chrift.* Thefe
eight examples, therefore, are made the fubject of the
prefent letters, in which they are regularly difcuffed in
order, as to the manner in which they were read and
underftood by the antient Fathers.† In making this
examination, to the extent which we have already mentioned, the moft important refults were found, as might
be expected, in the writings of the Greek Fathers: and,
as we have ftated the appeal to their accurate knowledge
of their own language as the chief object of thefe letters,
we fhall, in our report upon them, pay little attention to
any other authorities.

"1. The firft of thefe eight examples adduced by Mr
Sharp‡ is Acts, xx. 28; but, as this is not applicable
unlefs τȣ Κυριȣ και Θεȣ can be proved to be the genuine
reading, which is very doubtful,§ it is paffed over in
thefe letters.‖ But the queftion concerning the right
reading ftill remains open.

2. "The fecond example is Ephef. v. 5, ουκ εχει κληρονο-
μιαν εν τη βασιλεια τȣ Χριςȣ και Θεȣ,¶ rendered, in our
common

---

* "The remaining example, which is the third in
order, has no operation of that kind, and feems to be
introduced chiefly for the fake of eftablifhing the reading
πνευμαλι Θεȣ, from the Alexandrian and other MSS. in
Philip. iii. 3. See p. 31, 2d edit."

† "They are fet down together at p. vi."

‡ "P. 27, fecond edit."

§ "Bengelius notices this reading, but marks it with
ε, one of his figns of difapprobation."

‖ "See Letter II. p. 12."

¶ "Sharp, p. 30."

common tranflation, ' hath any inheritance in the kingdom of Chrift and of God;' but, according to the rule
of conftruction laid down by Mr Sharp, ' in the kingdom of the Chrift and God;' or, according to an explanatory fubftitution, ufual with our tranflators in other
cafes, ' of Chrift, *even* of God;' meaning that it is one
and the fame perfon who is here called both Chrift and
God. The examination here taken up * is, whether this
text was fo underftood by the Greek Fathers, or in any
other way. The conclufion is, as this author tells his
correfpondent, ' that no other interpretation than *yours,*
(Mr Sharp's) was ever heard in all the Greek churches.'
The paffages that moft remarkably prove this (for we
cannot be expected to cite them all, or to notice the in-
cidental difcuffions†) are the following: 1. A paffage in
the fifth Homily of St Chryfoftom, on the incomprehen-
fible nature of God, where this text is cited, with three
other of the ftrongeft fcriptural declarations, to fhow that
Chrift is God. 2. A paffage from Cyrill of Alexandria,
who, after quoting this verfe from the Ephefians, fays,
Ιδε παλιν Χριςον ονομασας ευθυς αυτον εκφερει και Θεον.
' Obferve, again, that, having named Chrift, he immediately adds, *that he is alfo God.*' In other parts of his
works, the fame Father cites this verfe, as denominating
our Saviour both Chrift and God, Χριςον αυλον ωνομαζε και
Θεον ἅμα λεγων. ' He calls Chrift himfelf God allo, when
he thus fpeaks,' namely, when he writes this verfe. 3.
The teftimony of Theodoret is no lefs explicit, for he
cites this verfe, with that to Titus, (ii. 13,) and others,
exprefly for the fake of proving that Chrift is God ; and
in one of the paffages inadvertently fubftitutes Χριςε τε Θεε
as perfectly equivalent to τε Χριςε και Θεε. Having given
thefe leading fpecimens, let us fum up the whole of what
is done, refpecting this verfe, in the words of the letter-
writer himfelf.

' We have referred to twenty-one Greek paffages in
which the words εν τη Βασιλεια τε Χριςε και Θεε are quoted.

Of

---

* " Letter II. p. 12."

† " Thefe are numerous, and the extreme candour and
caution of the author appear in every inftance."

Of thefe we confider twelve as determining nothing either
way with refpect to the meaning of thofe particular words;
but then we obferve, that it is not for the fake of thofe
words their quotations are made. The remaining nine
are, with one voice, clear teftimonies for your (Mr
Sharp's) interpretation. That is, in fact, all the Greek
authorities that do fpeak at all are on your fide.' P. 36.

" Much difcuffion is alfo taken up in this letter concerning the comparative value of the Latin writers, and
the weight of their teftimony when they are contrary to
the Greek: but this, which is managed with great judgement, we cannot repeat.

" 3. On the next example,* (2 Theff. ii. 12,) which
is the fubject of the third letter, it fo happens that there
are no decifive authorities. The verfe appears not in the
polemical writings of the Fathers, becaufe it contains
nothing decifive againft the Arians,† with whom their
chief controverfies were carried on: and they who wrote
continued commentaries faw no occafion to expatiate upon
words which to them appeared perfectly clear. This
example, therefore, does not long detain the writer of
the letters, who is careful, however, to remark, that
nothing appears againft the propofed interpretation, and
that feveral prefumptions ftrongly favour it.

4. " In the fourth example,‡ (1 Tim. v. 21,) we are
again in part deferted by the reading of the text, the
citations of the Fathers being made in general without
the

* " The third here, the fourth in Sharp, (p. 34,)
tranflated by him, ' according to the grace of Jefus
Chrift, our God and Lord."

† " Who allowed the Divinity of Chrift, which this
verfe afferts, but conceived his Godhead to be of a fe-
condary kind, againft which it fays nothing. Had it
placed Chrift before the Father it would have been often
cited."

‡ " The fifth in Sharp, p. 38."

the important word κυριυ,* thus removing it from any
application of the rule. It ftill, however, remains to be
inquired which is the proper reading of the verfe, by
means of MSS. and verfions; a fearch which the prefent
author does not fully undertake, (as being foreign to his
immediate object,) but touches with great judgement.
Mr Sharp fays that the word Χριςυ is omitted in the Alexandrian MS. contrary to the authority of Wetftein and
Griefbach, who affert it of κυριυ. We have examined
the MS. itfelf, and find that Mr S. is in this inftance
miftaken, and that κυριυ is the word omitted, the text

being ενωπιον ΤΟΥ ΘῩ ΚΑΙ ΧῩ ΙῩ, which are the undoubted abbreviations of Θευ και Χριςυ Ιησυ." [This
error is corrected in the prefent edition, fee note, p. 38
to 40.]

" On this paffage alfo occurs the only apparent contradiction of Mr Sharp's rule which the whole refearch has
produced, in three citations, namely, from Chryfoftom,
Œcumenius, and Theophylact, in which τυ Θευ και κυριυ
is retained, and yet the words are interpreted of two
perfons. As the only folution of this difficulty, Mr
Wordfworth fuggefts that the MSS. of thefe writers had
not κυριυ, which, with refpect to the two latter, appears
probable. But here he does not quite retain his ufual
acutenefs; for, Chryfoftom (unlefs it be an error of the
prefs in this book) muft have had κυριυ, as he has, peculiarly to himfelf, the additional word ημων fubjoined.
But it may fairly be conjectured that he read it και ΤΟΥ
κυριυ ημων, which, by inferting the article again, equally
removes it from the influence of our rule. As a col-
lateral proof (and a very ftrong one it is) that the

L   inconfiftency

---

* " Thus: ενωπιον τυ Θευ και Ιησυ Χριςυ, which makes
it no longer an example of Mr Sharp's rule. The common reading is τυ Θευ και κυριυ I. X. On looking back to
our article on Mr Sharp's book? (vol. xv. p. 71,) we
perceive, that, in the hurry of a periodical prefs, we
ourfelves have omitted κυριυ: a moft material error. Alfo
την before Χαριν, in the preceding text.

inconfiftency of conftruction, apparently found in thefe three paffages, cou'd not really belong to them, this author obferves that fimilar phrafes in the fame three Greek Fathers,* and the very words ὁ Θεος και κυριος, in twenty-fix citations from others, are uniformly referred to one perfon.

" 5. The fifth example,† (2 Tim. iv. 1,) which is nearly in the fame words as the preceding, fhares a very fimilar fate, being removed from the influence of the rule by the repetition of the article τȣ Θιȣ και τȣ κυριȣ. Mr Sharp, however, alleges that τȣ Θιȣ και κυριȣ is the reading of the Alexandrian MS. But the text of that

MS. gives, as in the former paffage, ΤΟΥ Θ͡Υ ΚΑΙ Χ͡Υ Ι͡Υ, τȣ Θιȣ και Χριϛȣ Ιησȣ." [This error is alfo corrected in the prefent edition, fee note, p. 38 to 40.] " It remains, therefore, to confirm the reading he fupports by other authorities." [For which fee note in 3d edit. p. 42—47.]

" 6. If we have had difficulties refpecting the readings of fome of thefe examples, we fhall have none in that to which we are now arrived.‡ It is that in the Epiftle of St Paul to Titus, (ii. 13,) επιφανιαν της δοξης τȣ μεγαλȣ Θιȣ και Σωτηρος ἡμων Ιησȣ Χριϛȣ: a text of which the read-ing is unitorm, and the interpretation of the Fathers exactly confiftent with that at prefent under confideration. The text was urged by them, in general, againft the Arians; nit to prove that Chrift is God, for that was granted by both parties, but to prove that his Godhead is

not

---

* " It is a very fingular and curious proof of diligence that the author of thefe letters fhould be able to fay (even with the modefty he obferves in it) of four fmall words, ὁ Θεος και κυριος, that they occur together but once in the twelve huge folios of Chryfoftom. The one paffage in that writer is τον κοινον ἡμων Θεον και κυριον τον Χριϛον. A very ftrong one in all refpects. See p. 56."

† " Sharp's 6th, p. 39."

‡ " Mr Sharp's 7th Ex. p. 42. Of thefe letters the 5th, p. 65.

not inferior to that of the Father, becaufe the Apoftle
here calls him the " GREAT GOD." To this argument
it was indifpenfably neceffary that the paffage fhould be
underftood according to Mr Sharp's tranflation, ' the
appearance of the glory of our GREAT GOD and
SAVIOUR, JESUS CHRIST;' and not according to our
public verfion, ' the great God, AND our Saviour Jefus
Chrift.'

" On this text the authorities are fo decifive that we fhall
content ourfelves with recounting their numbers inftead of
eftimating their force. The Greek authorities are fifty-
four in number, as cited in thefe Letters,* and extend
from the fecond century to the twelfth, a period of nearly
a thoufand years. In this inftance, alfo, the Latin fathers
and divines bear the fame teftimony, with very few and
inconfiderable except ons, and are cited to this effect in
about fixty inftances. Even the heritics of the Latin
church, till very late times, acknowledged the interpretation contended for by Mr Sharp; and that adopted in our
public verfion ' was never once thought of in any part of
the Chriftian world, even when Arianifm was triumphant
over the Catholic faith. , Surely,' adds the author of
thefe Letters, and we heartily add with him, ' this fact
might of itfelf fuffice to overturn every notion of an ambiguity in the form of expreffion.' P. 95. The perfect eftablifhment even of this one text, in the fenfe here afcribed to
it, if that were all that could be done, ought to give the
Socinian fome apprehenfion, when he prefumes to degrade
to the rank of a mere man, him whom the Apoftle Paul
unequivocally ftyles ' the GREAT GOD.' We believe,
indeed, with the author of the Letters, that even the
leaders of the fect have had their fecret compunctions on
this fubject.†

" 7. Of the two remaining examples we muft expect to
find lefs illuftration. The Catholic Epiftles were lefs
quoted, and lefs commented upon, than thofe of St Paul;

and

---

* " And the author fhows that he could have increafed
them."

† " See p. 66."

and even Chryfoftom, voluminous as he is, deferts us
when we come to the fecond Epiftle of St Peter. The
feventh example* is taken from that Epiftle, 2 Pet. i. 1.
Εν δικαιοσυνη τυ Θευ ημων και Σωτηρος Ιησυ Χριτυ, that is, in
the common verfion, ' through the righteoufnefs of God †
and our Saviour Jefus Chrift:' in Mr Sharp's rendering,
' through the righteoufnefs of our God and Saviour, Jefus
Chrift.' The authorities of the Fathers, both Greek and
Latin, are here neutral; but it is fomething of importance
to our inquiry, (which is noted by Mr Sharp,) that
Wickliff, Coverdale, Matthews, Cranmer, the Geneva
and Rhemifh Bibles, Doddridge, Scattergood, Wefley,
and Purver, all tranflate the words according to his rule.

" 8. We come now to the laft of thefe examples, Jude,
ver. 4, τον μονον δεσποτην, Θεον, και κυριον ημων, Ιησυν
Χριτον, αρνυμενοι,‡ ' denying our only Mafter, God, and
Lord, Jefus Chrift.' Here is fome difficulty in the reading, Θεον being wanting in many MSS. The chief teftimony adduced is from fome fcholia of the 11th century,
publifhed by Profeffor Matthæi, which conclude οτι εις
εστιν ο παλαιας και νεας διαθηκης Θεος και κυριος, Ιησυς Χριτος.
' That there is one Jefus Chrift, the God and Lord of the
Old and New Teftaments.'

We fhould here finifh, but that the author of thefe
Letters has fuggefted a new paffage as belonging to the
fame interpretation, though not to the fame rule.§ This
is James, i. 1, Ιακωβος Θευ και κυριυ Ιησυ Χριτυ δυλος, where,
though the article is not prefixed to Θευ, it is thought
probable, and by fome proofs much confirmed, that the
Apoftle meant to ftyle himfelf, ' a fervant of our God and
Lord, Jefus Chrift.' The author concludes his collection
by

---

* " Sharp 8th, p. 44. Letter VI. p. 103."

† " Erroneoufly printed, in Mr Sharp's remarks, ' of
our God.' P. 45, 2d edit." (Corrected 3d edit. p. 51.)

‡ " Sharp's Ex. 9, p. 46. Letters, p. 108."

§ " See alfo Rev. xix. 17, if the true reading there
fhould turn out to be δειπνον τυ μεγαλυ Θευ, inftead of
δ. το μεγα τυ Θ. See p. 66."

by various paſſages, from twenty different Greek writers, exemplifying the alleged uſe of the article, and many of them ſtrongly declaring the Godhead of Chriſt.

"Thus have we completely ſhown the ſubſtance of the information contained in theſe Letters. It is extremely important; and, though the candour of the letter-writer prevents him from attempting to take advantage of any dubious text or readings, the whole maſs of evidence which he has collected is abundantly ſtrong and valuable. The work is rendered of additional value by ſupplemental tables of the Greek and Latin Fathers, placed in chronological order, with ſome account of their extent and of the editions uſed by the author. We cannot conclude without recommending to every diligent ſtudent in divinity to read both this book and that of Mr Sharp, to confirm themſelves in that doctrine of which the primitive church never entertained a doubt,[*] the ' DIVINITY OF our BLESSED SAVIOUR.' Nor ſhall we attempt to conceal, that we view with great pleaſure theſe rational endeavours to ſupport a doctrine ſo fundamental to our religion."

—◆—

Review of G. Sharp's Remarks on the uſes of the Definite Article, and on the Six Letters to G. Sharp, in the CHRISTIAN OBSERVER for July, 1802. No. VII. vol. i. p. 438, art. xxvii.

After reciting the firſt rule propoſed by G. Sharp, the learned reviewer remarks,

"This rule is valuable, not merely in a philological view, but becauſe it enables us to correct the tranſlation of ſeveral paſſages in the New Teſtament, which, properly underſtood, afford "many ſtriking proofs concerning the godhead of our Lord and Saviour Jeſus Chriſt." Under this idea we are referred to the following paſſages. Acts, xx. 28. Eph. v. 5. 2 Theſſ. i. 12. 1 Tim. v. 21. 2 Tim. iv. i. Titus, ii. 13. 2 Pet. i. 1. Jude, 4.

---

[*] "Notwithſtanding the daring aſſertions that have, in modern times, been made to the contrary."

"The

" The Six Letters addreſſed to G. Sharp, Eſq. (which
we have heard attributed to the Rev. C. Wordſworth, M. A.
and Fellow of Trinity College, Cambridge) may be conſidered as an important ſupplement to his work. It ſeems reaſonable to ſuppoſe, that, if Mr Sharp's rule be true, the antient interpretations of any particular example by the Greek
fathers muſt tend to confirm it. The objeċt of this work,
therefore, is to examine, by actual reference, what were the
opinions of the early Greek writers upon thoſe eight texts
which are mentioned above. In the courſe of this learned ·
and moſt laborious inveſtigation, the author not only
proves, by a great variety of quotations, in what ſenſe
the fathers underſtood theſe paſſages, but ſhews, farther,
at what time and amongſt what writeis the interpretation
began to be ambiguous. To any one at all converſant
with the Latin and Greek languages it cannot be a matter
of aſtoniſhment, if, for want of the definite article, an
ambiguity frequently occurs in the Latin tranſlation of a
Greek ſentence, where there is no difficulty whatever in
the original. And to this ſource the author traces the
uncertainty which has ſo long exiſted with reſpect to the
true meaning of the texts cited by Mr Sharp. Few of
the Latin fathers were converſant with Greek ; they
quoted in general from their own tranſlations, and therefore generally adopted that ſenſe which, to a mere Latin
reader, would appear the moſt obvious. If, then, the
Greek and Latin writers ſeem to differ with reſpect to the
meaning of a Greek paſſage, the queſtion to us becomes
this : " Shall we take the explanation of a Greek paſſage
from Greeks or prefer from Latin writers, not the explanation of the Greek, but of a *tranſlation* of it into their
language ; which tranſlation, though capable of *both* mean-
ings, and ſo originally not a falſe tranſlation, would much
more naturally lead men to that ſenſe which is contradic-
tory to the common Grecian idiom and the uniform voice
of Grecian interpreters ?" p. 38. As our limits will not
allow us to follow this author through his numerous and
truly valuable quotations, let it ſuffice to ſtate the general
reſult. It appears, then, that where there is no reaſon to
ſuppoſe a different reading obtained from that adopted by
Mr Sharp, the Greek writers are deciſive in ſupport of

his

his interpretation; the contradictions and ambiguities rest with the Latin writers. In the second, fifth, and sixth, Letters, the quotations are numerous and highly satisfactory: they prove, incontestably, that words arranged according to the rule never did, from the times of the Apostles, bear any other sense than that assigned by Mr Sharp during the period while the Greek was a native language. This remark is not to be understood as applicable merely to the verses in question, but as extending to this mode of expression wherever it is used. In proof of this assertion, a considerable number of passages is here produced from the earliest fathers down to the thirteenth century: and the author adds, " I have observed more (I am persuaded) than a thousand instances of the form " 'Ο Χριςος και Θεος," (Ephes. v. 5); some hundreds of instances of the " Ο μεγας Θεο, και Σωτηρ," (Tit. ii. 13.); and not fewer than several thousands of the form " Ο Θεος και Σωτηρ," (2 Pet. i. 1.); while in no single case have I seen (where the sense could be determined) any one of them used, but only of *one* person." p. 132. Nay, the Arians themselves, it should seem, even at a time when their heresy was triumphant, acknowledged this construction, in admitting that Christ is styled, by St Paul, the great God. The words of Maximin, the Arian Bishop, as cited in this work, (p. 95,) are very remarkable:
" *A nobis unus colitur Deus, innatus, infectus, invisibilis, qui ad humana contagia, et ad humanam carnem non descendit. Est autem et filius secundum apostolum, non pusillus, sed* magnus *Deus. Sicut ait beatus Paulus :*" " *Expectantes beatam spem et adventum gloriæ magni Dei et Salvatoris nostri Jesu Christi,* &c. They did not deny that Christ is here called the great God, but contended that the Father was greater.

Towards the close of his work the author suggests some philological remarks, which well merit attention.

We cannot dismiss this article without offering a few remarks upon the subject which this work is meant to examine. The rule laid down by Mr Sharp was originally proposed by Beza: his words relating to the passage in Titus are the following: " *Quod autem ad alterum attinet, quum scriptum sit,*" " επιφανιαν τω μεγαλω Θεω και Σωτηρος

Σωτηρος ημων Ιησυ Χριςυ, non autem, "του μεγαλου Θεου και ΤΟΥ Σωτηρος," &c. dico non magis probabiliter ista posse ad duas distinctas personas referri, quam illam locutionem, "ὁ Θεος και πατηρ Ιησου Χριςου." Nam id certe postulat Græci sermonis usus, quum unus tantum sit articulus, duobus istis nempe, "Θεου και Σωτηρος" et "Θεος και πατηρ" communis." The rule, however, not being laid down with sufficient accuracy, and a due regard to the exceptions of a proper name and a plural number, Erasmus and Grotius paid little regard to it. Since that period it has often been asserted or denied, according to the preconceived opinions of different writers ; it has been generally admitted that it *might* be true, but contended on the other hand that it might also be false. Mr Sharp was the first who laid down the rule with clearness and precision, declaring that words thus arranged *must* bear this construction, and *can* bear no other. The public have now been for some years in possession of it ; and we believe it has never yet been controverted by any man. The rule must have been known to his learned Editor, Mr Burgess, some time before ; yet it seems a fair presumption that no exceptions have come under his notice, for he has lately published a second edition of the same pamphlet. ▸ The information contained in the Six Letters is calculated to give the strongest support and most ample conformation

---

▸ "We have heard the question advanced, " Does Mr Sharp's first rule obtain in the Septuagint and classical Greek writers ? " This mode of expression does not often occur in the LXX. ; but where it does occur, we believe, all the instances are in favour of this construction ; if we mistake not, the first example which can be produced is in Levit. xxi. 10. In the writings of the Greek classics we have noticed hundreds of instances, and have not yet seen one which makes against the rule. Take an example or two : "Οι δε, ατε ου δωροδοκοι οντες, καταφρονουσιν απαντων τουτων, ως φησιν Ο Θεος ΚΑΙ Θειων προφητης (viz. Homer:) Plato's 2d Alcibiad. Και γαρ τοι πεμψαρ Ιππονικον Ο συμμαχος ΚΑΙ φιλος αυτοις Φιλιππος. (Demosth. κατα Φιλιππου, Λογος γ.)"

to the rule. In this view, therefore, we confider this work as of very great importance; it enlifts into the fervice of the catholic faith feveral texts which have been frequently claimed by Arians and Socinians, as exclufively in their favour; thus depriving herefy of one of its greateft ftrong-holds, and affording another proof of the doctrine of the Trinity, which it will not be eafy to elude.

"Feeling, as we do, the fulleft conviction, that a body of evidence is here brought forward which the adverfaries of our faith can neither gainfay nor refift, we challenge them to the examination of it. if Mr Sharp's rule be falfe, let them prove it by an appeal to the Greek Teftament; if the quotations in thefe Letters can bear any other conftruction than that which the Author gives them, let another interpretation be produced. Till this fhall be done, and we are perfuaded it never can be done, we do moft earneftly recommend this learned work to all thofe who are able to appreciate the value of fuch evidence, and are defirous to "contend earneftly for that faith which was once delivered to the faints.

"For the fake of the mere Englifh reader, we fubjoin a tranflation of the paffages mentioned by Mr Sharp, according to his rule, and the interpretations of the Greek fathers: we omit the firft and fifth, becaufe the reading in our common editions of the Greek Teftament is different from that adopted by Mr Sharp.

"Ephef. v. 5. 'For this ye know, that no whoremonger, &c. hath any inheritance in the kingdom of him who is Chrift and God.'

"2 Thef. i. 12. ———'according to the grace of Jefus Chrift, our God and Lord.'

"1 Tim. v. 21. 'I charge thee, before Jefus Chrift, the God and Lord,' &c.

"Titus, ii. 13. 'Looking for that bleffed hope, and the glorious appearing of Jefus Chrift, the great God and our Saviour.'

"2 Pet. i. 1. 'Through the righteoufnefs of Jefus Chrift, our God and Saviour.'

"Jude iv. 'And our only Mafter, God, and Lord, Jefus Chrift.' "

The

, The reader is requested to examine also a very learned,
sensible, and candid, review, in answer to Mr Blunt's
Six more Letters to G. S. on the same subject, in the *Christian Observer* for June, 1803, No. vi p. 363.

CHRISTIAN GUARDIAN.

Extract from the CHRISTIAN GUARDIAN, for December, 1802, Number XII. p. 348.

' " Remarks on the Uses of the Definite Article in the
Greek Text of the New Testament, &c by Granville
Sharp, Esq.: to which is added an Appendix, containing,
1. A table of evidences of Christ's divinity, by Dr
Whitby ; 2. A plain argument from the Gospel History
of the divinity of Christ, by the editor, the Rev. T. Burgess, Prebendary of Durham. pp. 80.

' " The new species of argument which is here so happily adduced, and addressed to the learned world, in support of the doctrine of our Saviour's divinity, not only
merits the grateful attention of its friends, but imperiously
demands the diligent scrutiny of its most inveterate enemies. It approaches so nearly to mathematical demon-
stration that we conceive it to be absolutely incapable of
confutation The school of Socinus was never attacked with
a more formidable weapon ; and it is with pleasure we see
this treatise particularly recommended, in the preface, to
Mr Wakefield's most deliberate consideration.

' It would be impossible for us, in our analysis, to do jus-
tice to the elaborate work before us, without transcribing
a very considerable portion of its invaluable contents.
We will, however, communicate so much as may enable
the judicious part of our readers to form a true estimate
of the force of the arguments employed, and excite in
them a powerful desire of becoming acquainted with it at
full length."

After reciting the rules and referring to the examples,
the learned Reviewer makes the following observation, in
p. 350, on the Appendix :

' " Mr Burgess's plain argument, from the Gospel history, for the divinity of Christ, is drawn up by way of
question

the thoufands of readers of Greek produce a few inftances[*]
to contradict the rule, and then will be the proper time to
confider whether or no it muft be given up for ever.

"The conclufions, however, which Mr Sharp has drawn
with regard to the interpretation of thofe texts of the
New Teftament above referred to, feem, in general, to
be fecured within a fecond wall by the interefting, and
we will fay *furprifing*, refult of the inveftigation of the
laborious author of the " Six Letters." The general
object of which work is, to arrive at thofe fame conclufions by another road; to eftablifh the fame truths by a
fecond perfectly diftinct train of reafoning. ' It occurred
to me,' (fays this author,) ' that I fhould probably find
fome, at leaft, of thofe texts, the vulgar interpretation of
which you have called in queftion, cited and explained by
the antient Fathers; not, indeed, as inftances of any
particular rule, but expounded by them *naturally*, as men
would underftand any other form of expreffion in their
native language.' If thefe interpretations, thus difcovered, fhould differ from Mr Sharp's interpretation, it
would feem to follow that his rule could not be true: if
they accorded with his, it would then feem that thofe conclufions muft now for a *fecond* reafon be admitted; and the
vulgar interpretation ought of courfe to be reformed
according to the ftandard of the primitive authorities,
This inference, however, would be ftill farther fecured,
if we fhould difcover, from our inveftigation, that thofe
heretics who were moft preffed with thefe paffages of
Scripture, while Greek was underftood as a living language, never devifed fo ready an expedient of eluding
their force as modern ages have perpetually had recourfe

---

* " As we confider the fubject which we are now upon
as of the very firft magnitude, we fhall be happy if any
of our readers will favour us with communications (fhould
they meet with them) to fuch effect. And we fhould be
equally glad to infert any additional citations in the
Fathers which may have efcaped the vigilance of the
writer of the " Six Letters;" or any particulars which
may tend to fupply the deficiencies, or remove the difficulties, ftill remaining in that inveftigation."

to,

to, viz. a pretended ambiguity in the form of expreffion in the original; — and if it fhould ftill farther appear, in other inftances, that the orthodox never betook themfelves to this alleged ambiguity, even in thofe cafes where it may be fhewn they muft, from their principles, naturally have been inclined to do fo.

" Upon this fimple and unobjectionable ground-work thefe letters are founded. The remaining five, after the firft, are principally occupied in laying before us, in a chronological order, the refult of the author's inquiries on each particular text; and they prefent an example of well-directed patience and perfeverance which has feldom been furpaffed. Almoft all the vaft remains of the Greek Fathers, and a great part of the Latin, appear to have been clofely examined; and, what is fcarcely of lefs importance, the labour feems to have been carried on, as the work is written, in a fober, cautious, and candid, temper. We cannot give a more correct general defcription of the work than by faying that it contains, as far as materials could be found, a hiftory of the interpretation of the texts in queftion, from the earlieft times nearly to the age of the reformation. With regard to more *modern* tranflators and commentators, Mr S. has given fufficient information in the latter part of his " Remarks." It is an important advantage of this hiftory that we learn from it not only what is true, but we difcover alfo the origin and progrefs of the falfe modern interpretation. The origin is undoubtedly to be traced to the imperfection of the Latin language; and the progrefs was accelerated and increafed by the great number of Latin commentators, by the greater familiarity of our early interpieters with thofe writers; perhaps, alfo, by the inclination to heterodoxy in Erafmus and others; and not a little, probably, by the referve and timoroufnefs of certain orthodox writers, forbearing and fearing to affert the true interpretation, not becaufe they themfelves did not hold it, but out of a love of peace, and becaufe they knew it was denied or difliked by others.

" Having mentioned Mr Sharp's conclufions, it feems but right that we fhould point out how far they appear to be eftablifhed, or otherwife, by this fecond inveftigation.

" In

" In the firſt, fourth, and fifth, inſtances, the readings in the Fathers do not correſpond with Mr Sharp's readings, and therefore the interpretation *is, as it ought to be,* different. In the ſecond it is proved, to our ſatisfaction, ' that no other interpretation than Mr Sharp's was ever heard in all the Greek churches;' and, farther, (what may ſeem ſtrange to thoſe who come to the conſideration of the ſubject only with modern ideas,) that, *if* they *could,* the Greeks *would,* (as the Latins *did)* have interpreted it otherwiſe. On the third example the quotations are leſs numerous and leſs ſatisfactory; ſufficient, however, when combined with a ſeries of other quotations, given in the fourth letter, to corroborate the general concluſion. The ſixth inſtance, by far the moſt important of all, is confirmed by a profuſion of evidence. The ſeventh and eighth have again little *direct* evidence; but what we have affirmed of the third is, we apprehend, true of them alſo.

" In the laſt letter a long ſeries of inſtances is given, tending to ſhew, that, from the very times of the Apoſtles, the identical forms of expreſſion uſed in theſe texts of St Paul, &c. were applied *perpetually* and *invariably* in the ſenſe which is agreeable to Mr Sharp's rule ; and hence proving ſufficiently in what ſenſe even thoſe writers who have not quoted them did underſtand, and would have explained and interpreted, the paſſages in queſtion.

" In this laſt letter, alſo, authorities are given which render it probable that the text of St James, c. i. v. 1, is to be added to thoſe in which our Saviour Chriſt is called God.

" Having thus given a view of the contents of theſe publications, we ſhall conclude with earneſtly recommending them to the notice of the public; and eſpecially to thoſe who have imbibed an inclination to Socinianiſm, to which ſyſtem a blow ſeems to be here given which muſt ſpread a ſickneſs through the whole frame. And, though far from being prejudiced in favour of novelties in divinity, we cannot but add that theſe works are, in our eſtimation, calculated to produce the moſt remarkable change which has long been witneſſed in the theological world; and as conſtituting together, though of ſmall ſize,

the

the moſt important defence of Chriſtian doĉtrines which this age, by no means deficient in ſuch, has produced. For, what is here done (if *any thing* be done) will have the remarkable diſtinĉtion of being done *once for all*, and muſt be not of a confined and temporary, but a univerſal and perpetual, efficacy."

In a Letter to the Editors of this Review, the reader will find a very juſt and ſenſible cenſure of Mr *Blunt's* SIX MORE LETTERS TO G.S. The ſaid letter is publiſhed in the ORTHODOX CHURCHMAN'S MAGAZINE for June, 1803, No. xxx; being the ſixth number of vol. iv. p. 347.

FOURTH APPENDIX,

In the matter of SHARP and BLUNT:

Conſiſting of Notes, with proofs and explanations tranſferred from the third preface by G. *Sharp*, in reply to the oppoſite pretenſions, titles, and allegations, ſet up by G. *Blunt*, Eſq. alias *****, alias *****, in his " *Six more Letters to G. Sharp.*"

❯❯—○—❮❮

Note the 2d, transferred from the third preface, p. 1.

" But all the other cenſures and allegations of Mr *G. Blunt* are ſo evidently *frivolous* and *groundleſs.*"*)

* Of the various remarks, by Mr Blunt, which may juſtly be claſſed under this head of *frivolous* and *groundleſs*, thoſe which relate to *the rules of Syntax* ſeem to demand the firſt notice in this place. In p. 6 and 7, (after much abuſe about " *awkward* and *confuſed manner*," — " *inaccuracy*," — " *inveloped in miſt and fog*," &c.) Mr *Blunt* thus charges G. *Sharp*: " Thus you ſometimes ſeem to confine

confine your remarks, to what you call nouns of perfonal defcription or application, fuch as Θιος, Παίηρ, Κυριος, Σωτηρ, &c. at other times you extend them, *without giving us any notice*, to nouns which are *mere names of things*, without any reference whatever to *perfons*, fuch as αμησς, Βρωσις, φως, γραφη, &c. as in pages 8, 10, 12, 13, &c." (referring to the 2d Edition.)

In p. 43, he renews this charge, " now, you, in your practice," (fays he,) " have neglected all thefe limitations, and have brought examples to confirm your rules, which violate every one of them. Thus, many of the examples", (fays he) " in your *fecond, third,* and *fifth,* rules, and the majority of thofe in the *fixth,* confift of nouns which are *not perfonal.*"

But thefe charges are entirely *groundlefs,* as far as they refpect the fuppofed introduction of nouns, which are not perfonal, or *mere names of things,* " *without giving any notice*";—becaufe it is expreffly declared in the body, both of the 2d and of the 3d rules refpectively, that " it denotes a *farther defcription of the fame* PERSON, PROPERTY, or THING, that is *expreffed by the firft noun ;*" and, in the fifth and fixth rules, not only *perfons* but alfo *things*, are *expreffly* included, fo that G. Sharp would really have deferved cenfure if he had not given fome examples of nouns which are " *not perfonal,*" or " *mere names of things*"; and, if Mr *Blunt* himfelf had not been " *inveloped in the mift and fog*" (to ufe his own words) of moft inveterate prejudices, he certainly would not have made fuch *groundlefs* objections.

Concerning the 3d rule, he objects in p. xii. that " it is not fpecified whether there is, or is not, to be an article before the firft noun." — But this omiffion is of very little confequence, becaufe Mr *Blunt* will find, on examination, (if he does not fhuffle from the point by fearching for evafions in the *Englifh* verfion, or by fetting up different rules of his own, formed from the *Englifh* fyntax, inftead of fairly examining G. *Sharp's* rules by the text of the *Greek* Teftament, from whence alone they were formed,) that, in either cafe, with or without the article before the firft noun, the rule has no exception, not even if we include *proper*

names,

names, which are expressly *excluded* from the first rule, so that the charge of *not giving notice* is entirely *groundless.*

ı Respecting the fourth rule, Mr *Blunt* objects in p. viii that it " *is very loosely worded;*"—but, as *nouns* of *personal description* are *expressly* excluded from it, there seems to be no need of any farther description.

His imitation of the 5th rule, from the *English* version in p. xiii and xiv, is extremely *frivolous,* not only as being a rule of his own forming, from the perversion of a mere *English* expression, which cannot reasonably be admitted as a proper ground of censure against a rule founded on no other syntax but that of the *Greek* testament; but also because his own example of it, viz. " *God and Father of* " makes directly against himself; for, if " *two different subjects* " were really intended, even the English idiom would certainly require the article *the* before the second noun, viz. " *God and* THE *Father of.*"

All this is the more especially *frivolous* and trifling, because he himself was aware that this *English* example of his was *defective.* (— " *The English Example* " (says he, in p. xiv.) " *which I have given as an illustration of this rule, though it exactly corresponds to the description required in the rule, will probably, to an* ENGLISH READER *conversant with such forms of expression, sound rather as a contradiction to the rule,* ") and his only reason for these miserable *evasions* seems, by what follows, to have been a vain endeavour to invalidate G. *Sharp's* example, taken from Ephes vi. 23. which, " *when understood or translated, as it ought to be,* " (says he, referring us " *for the meaning of this Text* " to his note in p. 158,) " *does actually contradict, instead of confirming, his 5th Rule, though he chuses to understand it otherwise.* " But, when we turn, as referred, to p. 158, we find only the bare mention of this Text, and *not* his translation of it; for, he leaves us to judge of what *his meaning* of it is by *his* gross *mistranslation,* in that page, of several other Texts, some of which G. *Sharp* had cited (p. 2, 2d Edit.) as examples of manifest supplications " *made to Christ, jointly with God the Father, for grace, mercy, and peace; all divine gifts, &c.* " But Mr *B.* has manifested a *wilful perversion* of all these plain Testimonies of Scripture against the Unitarian system, not only by his *ungrammat-*

ıcal

ical rendering of the firſt example given us in that page, (κατ' ιπιλαγην Θιυ Σωτηρος ημων και κυριυ Ιησυ Χριςυ "Thus," ſays he, ' 1 Tim. i. 1. ſhould be rendered'—" *according to* (not *by*) *the commandment of God, Saviour of us, and Lord of Jeſus Chriſt*;") but, alſo, by his having ſubſtituted 1 Tim. i. 1. for 1 Tim. i. 2. the former having never been cited by *G. Sharp,* for any ſuch inference about *joint prayer to Jeſus,* as it contains nothing of that kind, but only the latter, 1 Tim. i. 2. Χαρις ελεος ειρηη απο Θευ παἰρος ημων, και Χριςυ Ιησυ τυ κυριυ ημων, which Text, he was moſt certainly well aware, would more obviouſly, than the other, expoſe the fallacy of his *new ſyſtem,* if rendered, according to *his* conſtruction of all the other Texts there cited, viz. his making the ſecond noun ʼto *mean* the *ſame perſon* as the firſt noun, though there is no article before the firſt noun, nor, inſtead of it, no *omiſſion of the Copulative* before the ſecond, which would have the ſame effect ; and, therefore, this Text, according to Mr Blunt's *curious* method of tranſlating all the reſt, muſt neceſſarily have appeared in the following abſurd and *unſcriptural* form, to *match* the reſt of his *miſtranſlated* examples :—" *God, Father of us, and Chriſt of Jeſus our Lord.*" This is a literal ſpecimen of *his mode of tranſlating* all the other Texts ; and it is manifeſt that he was aware of this abſurdity, or elſe he would not have evaded it by citing, inſtead of the proper Text, the preceding verſe, from which G. Sharp never pretended to draw any inference about, " *joint prayer to Jeſus,*" for it contains nothing to that purpoſe.

As to his two other *miſtranſlated* examp'es in the ſame note, p. 158. viz. Tit. 1. iv.—*from God, Father and Lord of Jeſus,* and 2 Cor. 1. ii." *from God, Father of us, and Lord of Jeſus,*"—he muſt very well know, as a *Greek* ſcholar, that nothing could juſtify his attributing, in that manner, the two principal diſtinguiſhing nouns in the ſentence (Παἰρος and Κυριυ) to *one* and *the ſame perſon,* unleſs either the *article* had been *inſerted* before Πατρος, or elſe the *Copulative omitted* before Κυριυ; but, as neither the one nor the other is really the caſe, his mode of rendering theſe ſentences is not only *frivolous,* but miſerably *perverſe,* and contrary to the general mode of expreſſion by the ſacred writers of the New Teſtament, from whom alone G. Sharp's

rules

rules of Syntax were formed, and contrary also to their moſt general application of the word Κυριος to *Chriſt* in other Texts, which are clearly independent of any diſpute about theſe Rules of Syntax.

Mr *Blunt* objeΦts farther in p. xiii to the fifth Rule, as follows—" It is not ſaid," (he remarks,) " either in Mr *Sharp's* Table of Contents, or in his Remark, (page 12,) whether there is or is not to be an article before the 2d Noun."—But, certainly, this was not neceſſary in a Rule intended merely for the *Greek* tongue; for, as there is no article before the 1ſt Noun, it cannot make any difference in tranſlating, whether there is or is not an article before the 2d noun, and therefore it would have been ſuperfluous to mention it. And, with reſpeΦt to his other objeΦtions about *imperſonals* and *want of notice*, &c. before cited, he himſelf has ackowledged, in p. xiv. that the Rule has " *perſon and thing*" and he might have added even *name;* ſo that ample mention and *notice* ſeems to have been given of the *enlargement* of this Rule, and, (unleſs the edge of his literary *penetration* be totally *blunted* by Unitarian prejudices,) it is ſufficient, one would ſuppoſe, to have prevented his *groundleſs* cenſures! but it is *not* ſufficiently *enlarged*, it ſeems, for .the admiſſion of his looſe and vague conſtruΦtions, either of *Greek* or even of his more ſlippery ſamples of *Engliſh*, which cannot paſs or evade it; (ſo that the *Machine*, as he calls it, really *binds* and *ſecures* the true meaning of the Text more effeΦtually on this trial of it than the *manufaΦturer* himſelf ever expeΦted;) for, indeed, Mr Blunt's *Engliſh* examples are quite foreign to the ſubjeΦt, ſo that there can be no pretence for admitting them; and, as to *his tranſlations* of the *Greek*, his ſamples are not only contrary to the general idiom of the *Greek* tongue, but contrary also to the moſt general application of the title Κυριος throughout the whole *Greek* Teſtament.

Mr. *Blunt's* objeΦtions to the 6th and laſt Rule, in p. xv, are equally *frivolous* and *groundleſs*; for, he refers to the *Table of Contents* again, inſtead of *the Rule itſelf*, wherein expreſs notice is given, that it includes nouns, either of *perſon, thing, or quality;* ſo that the incluſion of *imperſonals*, in the examples of it, cannot with juſtice be condemned as

a

a deviation from it. Another equally *unjust* censure by Mr *Blunt* of the 6th Rule is in p. 43. " *In your 6th Rule*," (says he) " *we have an Example from John* xi. 44. *consist-ing of two* PLURAL *nouns ; and, again in the 3d Example, in page* 31 *we have,*" (says Mr Blunt) " *two* PLURAL *nouns taken from Philip.* iii. 3. *which you mark as a* CAPITAL *confirmation of your first rule.*" But G. *Sharp* has neither *marked* or *remarked* any such thing. G. *Sharp* has said, indeed, in page 6, as Mr *Blunt* himself has *remarked*, that, " *there are not wanting examples even of* PLURAL *Nouns, which are expressed exactly agreeably to the first Rule.*" On which Mr *Blunt* again remarks, that it is " *an observation made for no other purpose,*" (says he,) " *that I can discover, but that of insinuating that there is nothing in* PLURALITY SO INCOMPATIBLE *with your Rule, as to prevent even plural nouns from being some confirmation of its truth.* But G. *Sharp* could not surely have any such purpose, (with due submission to Mr *Blunt's penetration,*) because he had, just before, and even in the same sentence, *expressly excepted* nouns that are " *proper names*, or *in the plural number*" and declared, also, that, in these " *cases, there are many ex-ceptions.*" This was surely an ample reason for excluding them from the 1st rule ; so that Mr *Blunt's* censure on this head, also, is really both *frivolous* and *groundless*, as well as his censures of the first Rule itself, because it does not ac-cord with the common *English* expressions,—*the* King and Queen; *the* Husband and Wife; *the* Father and Son," &c. —nor with his own vain and evasive quotations from the *English* version of the Bible!

And, as he has not been able to produce against the Rules one single example properly applied to confute them from the *Greek* text of the new Testament, (the only true crite-rion of their truth,) his abusive censure of the Rules and of their Author, in p. xvi. must surely deserve some epithet still more *cutting* and severe than either *frivolous* or *ground-less ;* for, Mr *Blunt* has no right to take offence at this freedom of expression, which he himself has so liberally bestowed, howsoever *pungent* the retort may be.—" *These Rules and Limitations,*" (says Mr Blunt, p. xvi.) " *are deli-vered and supported by the original Inventor with a haziness, which few foggy, shuffling, Trinitarians have exceeded, and transgressed* '*tranfgreffed with a bold freedom, which few impious, or apoftate, Socinian Sadducees have equalled,*' &c.

Mr *Blunt*, perhaps, confiders this grofs abufe as a mere retort upon G. *Sharp* for having fometimes diftinguifhed the *Socinians* by the name of Sadducees; (for, that defcriptive term feems to have penetrated moft deeply into the wounded mind of Mr *Blunt*, and *whetted up* his refentment, if we may judge by the repeated mention he has made of it throughout his work;) but, as the propriety, or otherwife, of all cenfures ought to be weighed, in the firft place, by the confideration—whether or not they are true? and, fecondly, whether they have been applied perfonally, *by name*, to any *known* individual?—or, thirdly, only in a *general way* to the mere errors and falfe tenets of the perfons who profefs them? Thefe confiderations will enable every attentive and unprejudiced Reader of G. Sharp's remarks very eafily to judge and decide whether he has really merited any fuch grofs abufe! Though the applying to the *Socinians* the title of *Sadducees* feems to have been particularly cffenfive to Mr *Blunt*, yet he does not appear to be aware of the true meaning of the term *Sadducee*, or he could not, with the leaft propriety, have objected to the application of that character to the *Socinians*; becaufe he himfelf, their boldeft and moft adventurous champion, has repeatedly, throughout his work, openly and publicly profeffed the leading principle of the old jewfih *Sadducees*, which has alfo been notorioufly held by many other *Socinians* befides himfelf; viz. that of denying the *exiftence of Spirits*, either *good* or *evil!* — An opinion as entirely inconfiftent with the *Chriftian Faith* as it is with that moft important and interefting branch of *natural philofophy*, the ftudy and knowledge of our *own nature:* for, without the protection and guidance of the HOLY SPIRIT, we can neither hope to " *be* PARTAKERS *of the divine nature*," (according to *the exceeding great and precious promifes*" which we hold " *through the knowledge of him that hath called us to glory and virtue*" 2 Pet. i. 3 & 4,) nor will it be poffible for us to refift an otherwife unavoidable PARTICIPATION of the contrary nature of *Demons!*

(Note

Note the 3d, transferred from the 3d Preface, p. xix.

("Mr Blunt's unhappy want of *faith* in the doctrine of *Christ's* Divinity,* &c.")

. * In p. 153, where Mr *Blunt* is speaking expressly " *of our Saviour's Divinity,*" he calls it a doctrine " *repugnant to every thing in reason and nature ;*" and, in the next page (p. 154,) he boldly asserts, that it is " *generally contradicted by the whole tenor of Holy Writ.*" And, in a note in p. 151, Mr *Blunt* very *hardily* plunges on in the same *groundless* error, asserting " *that the Divinity of Jesus, upon which the Trinity depends, is denied and declared to be false by the Apostles, in terms as positive, direct, and explicit, as can well be conceived.*" But, the very first text to which he has referred us for this strange assertion, both in this note and in p. 154, (viz. John, xvii. 3,) bears ample evidence to the contrary ; for, though our Lord there addresses his heavenly Father as " *the only true God,*" yet this cannot imply (either in this Text or in any of the other Texts to which Mr *Blunt* has referred) that our Lord himself, though eminently "*the Son of Man,*"—"*the Son of David,*" —"*the Seed of Abraham,*" &c. is not also *truly God*; of the ONE *divine Nature*, "*Godhead,*" or Θεοτης ; because, in the same prayer, plainly and openly, (doubtless for the instruction of his faithful witnesses,) he asks to be *glorified* with his heavenly *Father* ; which he could not have done without being liable to the charge of a very criminal presumption, if he had not perfectly known that he himself was *truly God* as well as *Man !* And he demonstrated his eternal *pre-existence* and *divinity* by requiring, in the plainest terms, that the *glory*, which he asked in his *then* lately acquired *Human Nature*, should be the same *Glory* which he had with his heavenly Father " *before the world was ;*" and yet this is the same identical person whom Mr Blunt presumes to call " *a mere Man,— and nothing more, or he was a deception.*" p. 71. Such a contemptuous (and of course impious) declaration against one, who is not only truly " man," but also, at the same time, so much " *more*" as to be expressly called παντων Κυριος, " *Lord of all.*", (Acts x. 36.) and emphatically ὁ κυριος,—" *the Lord,*"

(equivalent

(equivalent to the *supreme* Title JEHOVAH, which laſt is alſo expreſſly attributed to him, *) could not proceed from the ordinary tenets of any Sectaries which ſtill profeſs to retain the *Faith* and general· *title of Chriſtians ;* but muſt be attributed to principles of downright *infidelity!*

In the ſame contemptuous ſtyle, (p. 144, note,) Mr *Blunt* propoſes the following queſtion, in anſwer to a Rev. Advocate for " *the Divinity of Jeſu ,*"—"Can he believe" (ſays Mr Blunt) " that the Diſciples of Jeſus ſhould con-verſe with him, as a *mere man,* ſhould ſee him live and die *like a man,* and afterwards be thus completely *ſettled* in the perſuaſion of his being the *Almighty God,* without leaving behind them ſo much as a hint of the *tranſition* of their minds from one opinion to the other, without taking the leaſt notice of the *means* by which a change ſo amazing was produced ?" But the propoſition is *fallacious,* being founded only on two *groundleſs* ſuppoſitions ;—the one, that the Diſciples conceived, like Mr Blunt, that *the Lord* was " *a mere man and nothing more ;*" and the other, that they *have not left behind them* ſufficient teſtimonies of his *Divine na-ture ;* for this whole quibbling argument hinges upon the required " *hint of the tranſition of their minds from one opi-nion to the other.*" The Diſciples, indeed, rightly con-ſidered their Lord as " *a man,*" but not as " *a mere man and nothing more ;*" becauſe they muſt have known, by the canonical Scriptures of the Jews, that the promiſed *Meſ-ſiah* ought to be of much ſuperior dignity ; and, therefore, even with reſpect to the Diſciples opinion of his *human nature,* Mr *Blunt* ought to have been aware, that, as proofs gradually occurred of the ſuperior and really *expected* cha-racter of the *true Meſſiah,* the diſciples did *not* neglect to' " leave *behind them*" ample and ſufficient declarations of their full conviction that he was really " *more than a man ;*" for ſuch is their open acknowledgement of his *divine* attri-butes " *Now are we ſure,*" ſaid they " *that thou knoweſt all things,*" &c.—" *by this we believe that thou cameſt forth from God.*" (John xvi. 30.) Let Mr Blunt, notwithſtand-

---

* G. Sharp proved this many years ago by abundant teſtimonies of Holy Scripture.— See his Tract on the Law of Nature and Principles of Action in Man, p. 230 to 294.

ing

ing his inveterate prejudices, carefully examine the extraordinary affertion of our Lord himfelf, in the preceding context, which occafioned this decided conviction of his followers. (See verfes 27 and 28.) And fo far was the opinion, refpecting " *the divinity of Jefus,*" from being " *denied and declared to be* FALSE *by the Apoftles,* in *terms pofitive; direct, and explicit,*" as Mr *Blunt* has FALSELY afferted, that, befides their very frequent *exprefs* declarations and teftimonies of his *divinity,* throughout the whole New Teftament, they actually *worfhipped him* after his *refurrection,* (Matth. xxviii. 9 & 17,) and *prayed to him* after his *afcenfion,* (Acts i. 24 & 25,) when he was *abfent* from them : [i. e. *abfent* in body, and outward, perfonal, appearance, but his *fpiritual* prefence was *always* with them, as promifed to all churches, or *congregations* of *faithful* believers, even where two or three *were gathered together in his name,* (Matth. xviii. 20,) a moft effential privilege of the *Chriftian Church,* which is totally inconfiftent with the *falfe* idea of Mr *Blunt,* and other *Socinians,* that he was " *a mere man, and nothing more* !"] And thefe acts of *worfhip* and *prayer* to Chrift would have been *idolatrous* offences to his *Almighy Father* if the Difciples had not been moft certainly convinced, that their *Lord Jefus* was truly *God* as well as *Man.*

Notes, No. 4, No. 5, and No. 6, transferred from the third preface, p. xvi.

(———alluding by frequent repetitions to his (G. *Sharp's*) being bred as a mere *tradefman,** (4th Note) *mechanic,* or *manufacturer†* (5th Note) ; whereas, on the other hand, Mr *Blunt* himfelf being fufficiently fenfible, no doubt, of his own *fuperior education‡* (6th Note), is manifeftly *inflated,* &c.)

* Note, No. 4.—" But you, Sir, a *dealer in Greek* in
" the fmall way," (fays Mr *Blunt* in p. 22,) " feem to
" think more highly of your *flock in trade* th n thofe
" who are more in the *wholefale line,*—no uncommon cafe,
" —and to imagine, as the *retail dealer* often does, that
" your *little commodity* contains fome fecret, myfterious,
" and extraordinary, virtues, not to be found elfewhere,

" or

" or by thofe who know more of *the article dealt in.* In
" *Greek*, at leaft, whatever may be the cafe in *Englifh*,
" you feem to fuppofe that a man may bid defiance to the
" *reafon*, and *common fenfe*, and *experience*, of all mankind,
" and make out any myftery he has a mind for."

‡ Now *G. Sharp* will not prefume to deny the pre emi-
nence of Mr *Blunt*, in the whole character of *fuperiority*
here defcribed ; for, whether it arofe from Mr *Blunt*'s
" *fuperior education*," or whether, as being " *a dealer in
Greek*" (as Mr *Blunt* fays) " *in the wholefale line*,"
either of *mifconftruction*, or of *groundlefs* affertions and
abufe, he has certainly far exceeded " *the retail trader*"
(*G. Sharp* himfelf muft allow) in " *bidding defiance to
reafon, common fenfe*, and *experience*," not only in *Greek*,
but alfo in downright, *plain, Englifh*, throughout his whole
work, as the feveral *famples* here cited demonftrate ! (See
Note the 2d, p. 124 to 130.

† Note, No. 5. — *G. Sharp*'s rules are diftinguifhed by
Mr *Blunt* as being " *wrought goods, or famples of his new
mode of manufacturing a God-man.*" (p. xi.) — *A mechanical power, which fhall fcrew down any writer of
Greek.*" (p. 25.) — " *Articular Straps*," (p. 39.) which
" muft be truly *fingular*, if they neceffarily and inevitably bind
" *whatever load you pleafe upon any number of individuals*,
" *making every one of them, as often as you catch him by
himfelf*," (which feems to be the unhappy cafe at prefent
with Mr *Blunt*,) " *apart from his fellows*, WILLY-NILLY
" *to fubmit, and, it may be, to become at once poor, and
maimed, and halt, and blind*," &c. (ftill *frivoloufly*
carping upon a mere *Englifh* phrafe, inftead of the only
point in queftion, the fyntax of the *Greek* Teftament,)
" *let him be ever fo well fitted* " (meaning, we fuppofe,
by his " *fuperior education*") " *and difpofed, in himfelf,
and ever fo loudly urged to refiftance*," [as he acknowledges himfelf to have been, " *or I fhould never*," fays
he, in p. 2, " *have fubmitted to my friend's fudorific ;*" fo that
his friend, it feems, the Editor, was the promoter, or
father, of " *the literary bantling*," according to one of
his own *blunt* expreffions, p. 1.] " *by all around him, yea,
though he be as ftrong as* SAMPSON, *and have the* PHI-
" LISTINES

" LISTINES *upon him to boot*;" &c. (p. 39.) But, though the rules were formed, indeed, rather in a *mechanical* way, as Mr *Blunt* infinuates, yet, as they were all formed from the fyntax of *Sacred Scripture*, in the original *Greek* tongue in which they were firft written, and not from any other *Greek* books whatever, (not even from the *Greek* Tranflations of the Old Teflament, which have not the authority of the original *infpired* writers, nor from *tranflations* into a *different* language, like the frivolous quotations from the *Englifh* verfion, which Mr *Blunt* has abfurdly oppofed to them,) but from the *fyntax* of the *Greek* Teftament alone, the more *mechanically exact* they have been drawn, according to the general *examples* of expreffion in the *original text*, the more *irreprehenfible*, furely, and *authoritative*, muft the rules be, (according to the moft effectual method of judging fcripture by fcripture,) to guide us in the true interpretation of all other fimilar expreffions, ufed by the fame *infpired* writers, who had frequent promifes, from their Lord, of fufficient help, by the guidance of the Holy Spirit :—" *He fhall teach you all things.*" (John xiv. 26.)—" *When he, the Spirit of Truth, is come, he fhall guide you into all truth.*" (John xvi. 13.)—" *He fhall receive of mine, and fhall fhew it unto you.* (John xvi. 14 & 15.)—" *For, the* HOLY GHOST *fhall teach you in the fame hour, what ye ought to fay.* "(Luke xii. 12.).

The repeated objections, therefore, of Mr *Blunt*, to the competency of fuch *infpired* writers, are not only *frivolous* and *groundlefs*, like his other arguments cited in a former note, but alfo *extremely wicked*, having no other foundation than his own *infidelity* and fhameful denial of the very exiftence of the *Holy Spirit !*

Neverthelefs, though he is apparently an *infidel*, yet, as he is fuppofed to be at leaft a *claffical fcholar*, —" *trained* " *to grammar from his infancy*," (p. 27.) his fruitlefs and vain endeavours to fet afide the rules muft be confidered as a ftrong evidence in their favour; for, though the firft rule has been well eftablifhed, by the fatisfactory proofs of it produced by the learned and candid author of the *firft fix Letters to G. Sharp*, yet the *manufacturer* of the *rules* was not completely aware of the importance and real value of *all the other rules*, until he had read the *fix*

more

more Letters of Mr *Blunt*, and obferved the laboured exertions of all the critical might and ftrength of this *Socinian Samfon*, to burft away from the rules, and to evade and flip out from the *mechanical* "*ftraps,—fcrews,—forcing irons*," &c. as Mr *Blunt* calls them; for, indeed, all the other *rules*, as well as the *firft*, feem neceffary to render the general conftruction of G. *Sharp's* MACHINE completely effectual to "*bind*" and "*hold faft*" all *unreafonable* cavillers, that happen to be caught, through their own vain attempts to oppofe it: for, Mr *Blunt* has notorioufly manifefted, in his own conduct, the fame *unreafonable excefs* of falfe zeal, in favour of his own *Socinian* prejudices, that he has attributed, in p. 93, to St. Jerome, in fupport of an oppofite doctrine, viz. that "*he would not "fcruple to violate all grammar, and to write what he avowed "to be barbarous and corrupt, to fupport*" (not, like *Jerome*, "*the Divinity of Jefus*," but, in the oppofite extreme of hardened prejudice to that which Mr *Blunt* has attributed to Jerome,) his own *infidelity*, and the *blafphemous* notions which proceed from it, however *accurate* he may be, as a *claffical* fcholar in other matters! All thefe abfurdities are evident marks upon him of his having been (as he fays) "*faft bound in mifery and grammar:*" (p. 26,) i. e. we muft fuppofe, by the tight fitting of the "*articular ftraps*" and "*iron fcrews*," for which he has expreffed fo much abhorrence, fo that, from his *neck* to his *feet*, (for, his *wandering* head and *vague* underftanding have not, indeed, been fufficiently fecured,) he muft have been grievoufly held in the "*yoke*," (p. 38.) *pillory*, (xix.) and "*ftocks*," (p. 29.) of G. *Sharp's mechanical* invention :— nay, "*the iron of the difcovery*" (feems to have) "*entered "into his foul*, (p. 29.) and "*the forcing irons*" have really been effectual to bind down this *Sampfon* of grammatical prowefs, not with any help of "*the Philiftines "upon him to boot*," as he has fuggefted in p. 39, but rather (as a much more likely cafe) with all his *Unitarian* brethren, *Mahometans*, and other *Philiftines*, on his fide, to affift him! For, he has luftily called out and appealed to the *Unitarian Tracts*,—*Taylor's Ben-Mordecai*,—and other partial and prejudiced combatants, to affift him throughout his whole agonizing conflict!

NOTES

NOTES—Continued.

—:o—

Note, No. 6, transferred from the third preface, p. xvi.

(———— through a confidence in his own superior education*.)

* Superior education, without a found *natural judgement*, will avail but little. Though Mr *Blunt* was probably " *trained to grammar from his infancy*," (p. 27,) yet
this *claffical* fcholar occafionally forgets the very firft rudi-
ments of grammar, (which " *every fchoolboy knows*," p.
78,) the due diftinction between a *fubftantive* and an *adjective*. For, in his objections, in p. 73, to one of G.
Sharp's examples of the 1ft Rule, viz. Ephef. v. 5, he
afferts, that the word Χϱιϛος " *is an adjective :*" for, he
had forgot to diftinguifh this Text from fome other Texts,
wherein the word Χϱιϛος has *the proper name* Ιησους added
to it ; in which cafe it may indeed be called a *verbal adjective ;* but, in this Text, and in a great multitude of
other Texts, where the *proper name* is wanting, the word
Χϱιϛος undoubtedly ftands as a *fubftantive* ; which *any little
fchoolboy*, even one that is bred for *trade* and *mechanics*,
could have told, from the very firft page of his accidence,
or Englifh grammar, viz. " *A noun fubftantive is that
" ftandeth by himfelf, and requireth not another word to be
" joined with him, to fhew his fignification*,"—which is
manifeftly the cafe with the noun Χϱιϛος, in Ephef. v. 5,
and in moft other Texts where it occurs ; and, 2dly, (Accidence, p. 2,) That " *a noun-adjective is that cannot
" ftand by itfelf, in reafon or fignification, but requireth to
" be joined with another word*," &c. So that Mr *Blunt*'s
curious remark upon this Text, in p. 73, that Χϱιϛος " *by
" the bye, is an adjective*," is furely a notable proof, againft
himfelf, of that very perverfenefs which he has attributed
to Jerome, in p. 93, that " *he would not fcruple to violate
" all grammar, and to write what he avowed to be bar-*

" *barous*

" *barous aud corrupt, in order to fupport*" his own unfcriptural prejudices !

He contends, repeatedly, that Θεος is a *proper name,* (p. 86, l. 25; p. 88, l. 10; p. 100 & 101; p. 111, l. 12;) though he himfelf clearly proves, in p. 132, that it is *not a proper name,* by its being applied to feveral different perfons as an appellation.—" *The title of* GOD" (has he) " *is an appellation, which even Socinians*" (be pleafed to remark,) " *without reading it in your texts, have* " *admitted, that the fcriptures have beflowed, not only upon* " *Jefus, but upon many other human beings.*" Nay, it is fo far from being a *proper name,* that he might have fhewn that it is applied, alfo, to the *Devil* himfelf; (*the God of this world,* 2 Cor. iv. 4;)—nay, even to the bellies of voluptuous finners ; (whofe GOD is their belly;) and, in his vain exertions to evade the rules, in p. 41, he requefts G. Sharp to fhew, that Χριτος, Κυριος, and Σωτηρ, as applied to *Jefus,* differ lefs widely from ὁ Θεος and ὁ μεγας Θεος than one *proper name* does from another ;"—and he informs us that Dr. Clarke calls " thefe nouns *charaεteriftical* " and *equivalent* (as it were) to *proper names.*" To all which, a plain anfwer readily occurs, viz. That they are all, indeed, " *nouns charaεteriftical ;*" i. e. nouns defcriptive of *perfonal qualities,* as G. Sharp has before afferted, but certainly not *proper names,* and, therefore, not *equivalent* to them ; which is proved by the regular diftinεtion made between fuch charaεteriftical nouns and *proper names* by all the writers of the Greek Teftament without exception ; and Dr. Clark, had he not been *darkened* by his own prejudices as well as Mr *Blunt,* muft have known the due diftinεtions between appellations (arifing from perfonal qualities, rank, or condition,) and *proper names :* and, though Mr Blunt himfelf has, alfo, repeatedly afferted that Θεος is a *proper name,* he has not yet been able to produce the leaft proof that it is fo; and, therefore, G. Sharp muft ftill confider it as a *perfonal* noun, defcriptive of *quality,* or rank, as well as the reft, differing only in the degree of quality ; and, of courfe, he muft ftill " maintain, "*that perfonal nouns,* EVEN OF THIS SORT, *are differently* " *affeεted by the article and conjunεtion from proper* " *names,*" (G. B.'s Rem. p. 42 ;) efpecially as G. *Blunt* has

has not been able, with all his moſt zealous exertions, to produce a ſingle example from the Greek Teſtament to the contrary. But, with reſpect to the *proper name* of G. Blunt himſelf, G. *Sharp,* though only a *manufacturer,* perceives much more difficulty ; for, though it is obvious that *Blunt* is not, really, his *proper name,* ſo as " *to mark an identity*" (as he ſays, in p. 38,) in the ordinary ſenſe and uſe of *proper names,* yet, in another ſenſe, the word *Blunt* may be conſidered, perhaps, as a *deſcriptive noun,* whether of his ungracious manners and rough addreſs, or whether, with reference to his *viſual organs,* which he calls upon G. Sharp " *to* PURGE with (his) *euphraſy,* " *and make them more* SHARP-*ſighted than they are at pre-* " *ſent ;*" or whether, ſtill, by " *a diverſity of references,*" (as he ſays,) it may allude to the *unpenetrating* defects of a mind, unhappily clouded, at preſent, by the darkeſt pre-judices of dangerous errors ; (for, we do not preſume to arraign his *natural mind* ; but, only, thoſe perverted pro-perties of it, for which he himſelf alone is moſt awe-fully accountable ;) ſo that, with reſpect to both theſe points,—of " *Identity*" and " *Diverſity of References,*" Mr *Blunt* has afforded us very conſiderable proofs, that *Blunt* is the *proper name* for ſuch a writer ; though we are convinced, at the ſame time, that he has aſſumed this name of *Blunt* merely for the preſent occaſion. And, though Mr *Blunt* declares, in p. 37,—' I CANNOT SEE' " (ſays he) what reaſon or authority you have for' " making theſe *fanciful limitations,* or for exempting ſuch " *nouns* (nouns not *perſonal,* or *proper names,)* any more " than others, from the operation of your rules." Yet, as Mr *Blunt* cannot produce a ſingle example from the Greek Teſtament, which can fairly be ſet ·in oppoſition to theſe *limitations,* he has, ſurely, no right to call them *fanciful* ; becauſe the facts deſcribed in the rules, reſpect-ing *nouns perſonal* and *proper names,* are really true, throughout the *general* ſyntax of the *Greek* Teſtament ;. and, though Mr *Blunt* CANNOT SEE them, G. SHARP is, ſurely, under no obligation either to " *purge his vi-ſual organs,*" (as he ſays,) " *to make them more* SHARP-*ſighted,*" to perceive the futility of his oppoſition to them, and the groſs abſurdity of his having recourſe to *mere*

Engliſh

English examples, for want of better proofs, against G. *Sharp*'s rules: as, for inftance, " *The king and queen ; the hufband and wife,*" &c. (p. 19,) as if thefe *English* expreffions could afford him any juft argument againft the ufual *Greek* fyntax, explained by the 1ft rule ; and, though he cites the fame *English* nouns, in p, 41, without the article before the 1ft noun, to " *exprefs diverfity*" (fays he) " *as ftrongly and as neceffarily as any proper names what-*" *ever can poffibly do* ;" yet, as he has here omitted the article before each of the two firft Englifh nouns, he cannot any longer oppofe them to the 1ft rule, becaufe he has here expreffed *the diverfity,* ftrictly, according to the terms of the 5th rule, which requires two diftinct perfons to be underftood. But, as both thefe *pairs* are, refpectively, only *one flesh* in law, his *diverfity* is, furely, very defective. But what has this to do with the *diverfity,* really required, between the *Greek* and *English* fyntax, though he refers, by an *et cætera,* to all thofe examples which (fays he) " *I mentioned in my former letter, and*" *many more that might be mentioned are as different* (fays he) *as* SHARP *and* BLUNT."——DIFFERENT, indeed ; for, when we " *compare the enormity of Mr Blunt's conclufions with the weaknefs of* (his) *premifes,*" we " *can*" *have no other alternative*" (as he fays, p. 137) " *but*" *to fuppofe, either a total want of reflection,*" or that his mind is fo clouded by the *habitual perfuafion* of his own *Unitarian* prejudices, " *that, as to inquiries of this fort,*" *it is become* (according to his own expreffion, p, 137 & " 138) *like the confciences Paul fpeaks of, perfectly feared*" *with a hot iron, and* (has) *loft all fenfe of feeling for*" *any thing but* (his) *own prepoffeffions upon the fubject :*" and, therefore, until he can recover a little more of the natural *acumen* and *penetration,* both of his mind and eyes, every attempt muft be ineffectual to convince him, that all the other examples, to which he has referred in his former letter, are equally impertinent as thefe to the fubject in queftion, and that mere *English* examples cannot afford any reafonable proofs againft the *Greek* fyntax.

In his third letter (p. 45) he fays, — " *I now proceed*" *to lay before you fome further examples of your rule, from*" *which*

" *which you will see more of the many admirable consequences*
" *of your discovery, than, perhaps, you were fully aware*
" *of. By the application of your rule* (probably meaning
" the first) *to the Greek text of the following passages, you*
" *may shew that there is no difference, not only between* A
" STREET *and* A LANE, (Luke xiv. 2.) *but between* A
" HIGHWAY *and* A HEDGE," (ibid. v. 23,) &c. &c.

And he cites a great number of other texts in the two
following pages, 46 & 47, which are quite as foreign to
the purpose of affording the least *just ground* of censure
against any of the rules, because he has totally disregarded
all the circumstances of syntax described in the rules, agreeable to his own notable resolution, professed in the beginning of that letter, viz. To " *set aside those limitations*
" *which* (says he) *I have* PROVED *to be futile and ground-*
" *less.*" But of *his* manner of PROVING I have already given a sufficient number of notable examples, under the head of " *frivolous and groundless;*" so that,
through this notorious *want of foundation* in all that he
has advanced, Mr *Blunt* is in danger of sinking over head
and ears in the *quagmire* of his own *groundless* censures
and absurdities.

Not a single text of all that he has cited affords the
least ground of *just* argument against the rules, unless the
same absurd liberties be admitted, of " *setting aside all*
limitations," according to his professed resolution ; and he
himself seems sensible of this ; for, in the last of the above
cited pages (47), he adds, " *but I shall content myself*"
(says he) " *with mentioning* ONLY ONE ;" so that all the
rest that he *has mentioned* just before are manifestly superflu-
ous, even in his own estimation. The text he thus particularly
mentions is 1 Tim. vi. 13, where " Θεος and Χριςος *being*
" *connected*" (says he) " *in the way your rule requires,* *the*
" *former with, and the latter without the article,* MUST
" NECESSARILY *be descriptive of one and the same person.*"
But, on the contrary, it turns out, that Mr *Blunt* has
condescended to furnish G *Sharp* with an ample reason
why it MUST NOT " *be descriptive of one person and the*
same person," viz. A *peculiarity of expression,* which with-
draws it entirely from the case described and intended
by the 1st rule : see the text,—Παραγγελλω σοι ενωπιον τυ
Θευ

Θεε τε ζωοποιεντος τα παντα, και Χριςε Ιησε τε μαρτυρησαντος επι Πονλιε Πιλατε την καλην ομολογιαν, &c. For, Mr Blunt, very properly, in *this one single instance*, remarks, that, *" since each of these nouns is attended by a participle, and " since the article, which is prefixed to the first participle, " is repeated before the second,* THE TWO *nouns must, on " that account, be descriptive of different persons.* In which remark G. *Sharp* perfectly agrees with Mr *Blunt*; being sensible, that the intervention of the participle and its article, and the repetition of the article, also, before the 2d participle, must render the sentence completely *different* from the common mode of expression, described by the 1st rule, and sufficiently explained by the first examples cited for it, from whence the rule was drawn, and of which the true interpretation has never been called in question, as they are not texts that are favourable to any particular controversy; and, therefore, the *very different form of expression,* above described, proves that this text of 1 Tim. vi. 3, (the *" only one "* text that Mr Blunt relied on, as a proof, to subvert the rule,) really affords no just argument or exception against it; and, consequently, demonstrates, that the conclusion he has drawn from it, about *identity* and *diversity,* is not only absurd, but (as it includes the mention of *God* and *Christ*) is extremely wicked!

Notes, No. 7 and No. 8, transferred from the third preface, p. xviii..

(——— as well as the more antient canonical writings of their *Israelitish* countrymen,* are of so *superior* a nature, in comparison with all other writings, even with those that are deemed most eminently *classical,* and are so very different in their general idiom and peculiarity of expression, that *rules,* drawn from the syntax of these sacred writings† —— &c.)

Note, No. 7. * The first promulgation or delivery of the oracles, or true revelations, of God belongs in a peculiar manner, it seems, to the *Jewish,* or (more properly)

perly) the *Israelitish*, nation; for, it is a very extraordinary circumstance, that all the true *prophets*, mentioned both in the Old and New Testaments, [except *Balaam*, who, as a stranger and enemy to *Israel*, was held under a very different and peculiar restriction and compulsion of God's power over him, to enforce his strict obedience to the *revealed* truth during the time he prophecied,] from *Moses* down to the last authentic, prophetical, Revealer of God's will, *John*, the beloved disciple of our Lord, were *all Israelites!* This extraordinary mark of favour to the Jews was declared by St. Paul, when, in answer to his own question—"*What advantage, then, hath the Jew?*" he said—"*Much, every way:* CHIEFLY, *because that unto them were committed the oracles of God.*" (Rom. iii. 1 & 2.)

This was, therefore, the *chief* and most *valuable inheritance* of the Jewish nation; because, the *possession*, or, rather, now, the *re-possession*, even of their former *temporal inheritance*, depends upon their attention and obedience to *these divine oracles and revelations* of their countrymen, in the *last* or *New Testament*, as well as in the First, by *Moses*, who, speaking of this very privilege, claimed it as their "*inheritance for ever!*" "The secret things (said he) belong unto the Lord our God; but those *things which are* revealed *belong* unto us and our children for ever, that we may do all the words of this law." (Deut. xxix. 29.)

Note, No. 8.

† All the sacred writings have an unusual style of expression, peculiar to the sacred books, and different from all other writings: but the *Hebrew* Scriptures are remarkable for an idiom or style still more particularly different than the rest from all other writings.

A little tract, to demonstrate this point, (written by the Author of these Remarks,) is now in the press, containing *Rules of Construction*, carefully proved by examples, drawn from the general syntax of the *Hebrew* Scriptures.

The *unusual style* of the Holy Scriptures, and the preference that is due to them, on the comparison with any other writings, howsoever learned and generally approved, is strongly marked in a sensible *French* work, printed at

Paris,

Paris, in 1626, entituled " Les Diverfitez Naturelles de
l'Univerfe, de la 'Création et Origin de toutes chofes."
p. 40 and 41. " Car, fi nous voulons porter reverence
aux autheurs ; — auxquels je vous prie en faut il porter
d'advantage, ou à l'Ariftote, Averrois, Epicore, et leurs
femblables, qui luifent feulement d'un petit flambeau de
doctrine humaine, ou bien à Moyfe, aux Prophetes, a
Salomon, le plus fage de tous ceux de fon fiècle, — aux
Evangeliftes et aux Apôtres, lefquel tous en fapience, en
fageffe, en mœurs, en propheties, en oracles, et en toute
forte de fainêteté, efclairent et flamboyent comme torches
ardentes, qui affeurent, D'UN STYLE INUSITÉ, ce quils
difent des chofes divines, le prouvent au peril de leur vie,
et le confirment par prodiges ? " &c.

Note, No. 9, transferred from the 3d Preface, p. xxi.

. (That Holy Men of God fpake as they were moved
by the Holy Ghoft, (2 Pet. xx. 21,) and not according to
their own will, as Mr *Blunt* feems to fuppofe, by his quotation from Dr Whitby, " *Scripffet ergo Judas fi hoc voluiffet*,"† &c.)

† So little does Mr *Blunt* regard the information we receive from the Holy Scriptures, — as cited above, and
elfewhere, refpeêting the *Guidance of the Infpired Writers
by the Holy Ghoft*, — that, as he could not find *real* texts in
the *Greek* Teftament to oppofe to G. *Sharp's* rules, (the
only fair method of confuting them if they had been
wrong,) Mr *Blunt's dark* prejudices have prompted him,
in p. 55, to urge the *fuppofed* confequences that *would*
arife to confute G. *Sharp*, if fome particular texts *had
been* written differently from what *they are!* for, indeed,
all his objeêtions are founded, in like manner, on *falfe
fuppofitions!*

In p. 46, he fays, — " *From Luke* viii. 1, 2, *You might
fhew, by your rule, that the twelve Apoftles were women*,"
&c. &c. But this, furely, is *not* by G. *Sharp's* rule, but
only by Mr *Blunt's* own abfurd manner of treating it ;
through the *unreafonable* refolution he had previoufly declared,

clared, in p. 44, viz. "*Looking upon myself, therefore, as quite at liberty, in arguing against your rule,* (says he,), *to disregard limitations, which I have shewn to be destitute of all foundation, and which you yourself have disregarded in your attempts to establish your rule, I shall now go on to give you the remainder of those examples,*" &c. This single sentence abounds with *false* suppositions: (1st,) That he, Mr *Blunt,* has shewn the *limitations* to be *destitute of all foundation*; a supposition which could only be founded on another *supposition* equally *false,* viz. (2dly,) that rules for the *Greek* syntax ought to be examined by *mere English* examples, (for, he has produced no others in his first letter;) and (3dly,) that G *Sharp* himself has *disregarded* his own *limitations,* an assertion, which Mr *Blunt,* with all his grammatical sophistry, cannot maintain; for, it is obvious that all the texts which he has cited in his second and third letters, *as objections* to the rules, are rendered so merely by his wilfully "*setting aside those limitations.*" See the first line of his third letter, p. 45.

In p. 48, he says, — "It makes no difference, I apprehend, in this reasoning, that the 'substantive of personal description,' as you call Χριϛος, (p. 30,) is followed by the proper name *Jesus*; since Χριϛος HERE" (he must mean in the text cited at p. 30) "does not make any part of the proper name, but is merely an epithet, like the similar personal noun κυριος, in a similar situation." All this argument is on the erroneous *supposition* that the text cited by G. *Sharp,* in p. 30, has the *proper name* JESUS, as well as "*the substantive of personal description,*" Χριϛος, (which, unluckily for his *careless* and *groundless* argument, happens not to be the case:) nevertheless, he adds, "*But what if it were, unavoidably, a proper name?*" But, without any *if* or other imaginary supposition, Mr *Blunt,* by his own fruitless attempts to make it a *proper name,* has proved that it is, *unavoidably,* otherwise, (and he has cited, in a note at p. 73, very ample authority, which he cannot reasonably gainsay, that it is NOT a *proper name.*) And yet he adds again, in p. 48, — "*Or, lastly,*" (says he, reserving his *clinching* argument for a conclusion, we will hope, of his vain suppositions,) "*what IF Paul had* THOUGHT FIT *to have omitted the word* JESUS *altogether, which he might*

O

have

have done if he had chofen it, for any thing that I can fee to the contrary?" — Thus Mr *Blunt* is thoroughly prepared to controvert whatever Paul may have written, by a *vain fuppofition* that he "*might have*" wrote otherwife "*if he had chofen it!*"—But, in this particular text, cited by G. *Sharp*, (p. 30, 2d edit.) to which he refers, *Paul* really has "*thought fit*" to omit the *word* J E S U S *altogether.* And yet Mr *Blunt's* argument is equally futile and vain; for, he had neglected to examine Paul's *Greek* as he ought, and unluckily formed his ideas, as ufual, from a mere *English* verfion of it, and that even by G. *Sharp* himfelf, the *manufaEturer*, who had fupplied the word *Jefus*, in a parenthefis, merely for the fake of explication! Oh! Mr *Blunt!* Mr *Blunt!*

But, in other *fuppofitions* which he has taken, even from the *Greek* text, his endeavours have been equally fruitlefs; for, in p. 55, he ferioufly warns us of feveral *fuppofed* confequences, that would arife from fome particular texts :—— IF *Mark*, for inftance, in one text, *had omitted* " *the article before the fecond noun*;" or, I F *John*, in another, " *had omitted both prepofition and article before the fecond noun*;" or, I F *Paul*, in another, " *had inferted the article before the firft noun*," &c.; or, " *Suppofe* " (fays he) " *Luke had told us*——" i. e. fomething different from what he really did write,—&c. &c. But, in drawing proofs from the *Greek* Teftament, we cannot furely have any bufinefs with fuch *idle fuppofitions* and trifling inconfiftencies; for, as neither *Mark* nor *John* have *omitted*, nor *Paul inferted*, nor *Luke expreffed*, any thing at all like his own vain *fuppofitions*, of courfe, all the texts that he has cited from them, as pretended *proofs* againft G. *Sharp's* Rules, (for, this is a true *fample* of Mr *Blunt's* method of *fhewing* that the *limitations* are *deftitute of all foundation,)* are completely contrary to his purpofe, and impertinent to the bufinefs in queftion; becaufe the rules convey the teftimony of what the Apoftles and Evangelifts *really did write*, in full anfwer to all Mr *Blunt's* abfurd *fuppofitions!* So that if G. Sharp's fecond " *correfpondent had paid more attention to this circumftance*," (i. e. the teftimony of what the Apoftles and Evangelifts *really did write*, inftead of his fuppofitions of what they *might* have written, *if* they had *chofen it,)* " *he would have underftood more*," (according to his

own

own *polite* obfervation, p. 84,) *" and mifapplied'lefs, of the rubbifh he has raked together !"*

Note, No. 10, transferred from the third preface, p. xxxvi.

(———— *" Drunk with the blood of the Saints, and with " the blood of the Martyrs of Jefus.*")

* This is a prophetical mark againft the *Roman* church, (the adopted ally of the *Socinians,*) a mark *too peculiar* to be miftaken ! efpecially as the farther mark of her nearly-approaching *judgement* is already come ; viz. That the Royal *Horns of the Beaft*, her fupporters, *" fhall hate* THE *"* WHORE, *and fhall make her defolate, and naked, and " fhall eat* HER FLESH," &c. (Rev. xvii. 16 ; a judgement which was firft begun by our Englifh *Horn*, K. Henry VIII. (whom fhe had intituled *" Defender of the Faith :"* i. e. *of her faith* againft the perfecuted *Saints :)* yet he fet the firft example of *" eating her flefh"* by the fequeftration of Ecclefiaftical Eftates and Revenues to the Royal Exchequer. This precedent, for fulfilling the prediction, was not followed by the other Popifh *Horns* of the Beaft, until the diffolution of the Order of *Jefuits*, in our own times, (about 1763 or 1766,) when all the other Popifh Kings of the *Roman* Empire, the Kings of *France, Spain, Portugal, Sardinia, Naples*, and the Emperor and *King*, Jofeph the 2d, &c. all followed the example ; and, laftly, fince the Treaty of *Amiens*, the remainder of *her flefh* feems to have occafioned a notable *Royal* fcramble among the remaining Royal *Horns*, under the general title of *Ecclefiaftical Indemnities* ; fo that, as *the fign* of the approaching vengeance is fo notorioufly fulfilled, the *judgement itfelf* cannot be far diftant, to punifh her *apoftacy*, and that of her prefumptuous *fecond hufband, Pontifex Maximus*, ὁ ανθρωπος της αμαρτιας, (2 Theff. ii. 3,) called alfo, *" the Little Horn,"* as being lefs in *temporal* power, than, all her other paramours, the *Horns* of the Beaft, and which, neverthelefs, the *adulterous* church blafphemoufly addreffes, by the *divine* title, of *" Sanctiffimus Dominus ;"* though her

her *firſt* Lord and Maſter ſtill reigns, in Heaven, and on Earth,—" *The Lord of Lord., and King of Kings!*" (Rev. xvii. 14, and xix. 16) So that he cannot be " *a mere man*" and " *nothing but a man,*" according to Mr Blunt's contemptuous aſſertions, in p. 151 and 173!

But the time is juſt at hand, when *Great Babylon* muſt come " *in remembrance before God, to give unto her the " cup of the wine of the fierceneſs of his wrath.*" (Rev. xvi. 19.) For, all the aweful ſigns deſcribed in this very text, the 19th verſe, though not yet *completely* fulfilled, are moſt evidently approaching to their completion. The *ten* greater diviſions (called *horns*, or *kings*) of the fourth and laſt great kingdom, the *Roman* empire, are now ſo *wounded* and, ſubdued, as to have an apparent tendency to be " *divided into three parts*" only, inſtead of *ten* parts or *horns:* and as to the other *ſign*, reſpecting the fall of " *the cities of the nations,*" mentioned in the ſame verſe, (and neceſ-ſarily to be underſtood as an *inferior* diſtinction for the *leſſer* governments or ſtates of the empire, which were not *regal* monarchies, or *horns* of the beaſt, but were deemed only *republics* and *hanſe towns* of the empire, therefore, properly, " *the cities of the nations,*") they are ſurely *already fallen!* Where now exiſt the *late* noble and inde-pendent ſtates of *Venice, Genoa, Switzerland, Holland, Bel-gium, Parma, Florence, (Etruria, or Tuſcany,)* or even *Ra-guſa!* becauſe none but the *piratical ſtates* exiſt, (reſerved, perhaps, for a more dreadful vengeance!) for, even *Bremen* and *Hamburgh* have been lat ly ſeized. So that the " THIRD WOE " really " *cometh quickly.*" O! that all *virtuous indivi-duals* of the *Roman* communion (for many ſuch undoubtedly there are) may ſincerely, and in due time, obey the divine warning,—" *Come out of her, my people, that ye be not par-" takers of her ſins, and that ye receive not of her plagues:*" for, " *in her was found the blood of prophets, and of ſaints, " and of all that were ſlain upon the earth.*" Rev. xviii. 4 and 24.

FINIS.

Printed by C. and W. Galabin, Ingram-court, London..